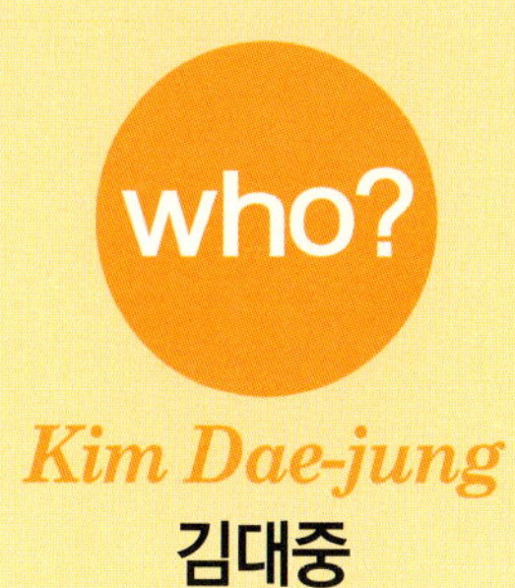

who?

Kim Dae-jung

김대중

Biography Comic
who? ㉚ Kim Dae-jung

개정판 1쇄 인쇄 2014년 3월 5일
개정판 1쇄 발행 2014년 3월 10일

글 이우정
그림 스튜디오 청비
번역 김성협
감수 김수희
펴낸이 김선식

책임편집 이유미 **디자인** 박효영
콘텐츠개발팀장 김선영 **콘텐츠개발팀** 박효영, 이유미, 김선민, 조서인
마케팅본부 이상혁

펴낸곳 스튜디오 다산 **출판등록** 2013년 11월 1일 제414-81-37694
주소 경기도 파주시 회동길 37-14 3층
전화 02-702-1724(기획편집) 02-703-1725(마케팅) 02-704-1724(경영관리)
팩스 02-703-2219 **who클럽** cafe.naver.com/dasankids
종이 월드페이퍼(주) | **인쇄** (주)현문 | **제본** 광성문화사

ISBN 979-11-5639-022-0 (14740)

• 책값은 표지 뒤쪽에 있습니다.
• 파본은 본사와 구입하신 서점에서 교환해드립니다.
• 이 책은 저작권법에 의하여 보호를 받는 저작물이므로 무단 전재와 복제를 금합니다.
• 이 책에 실린 사진의 출처는 드림스타인, 위키피디아, 연합뉴스입니다.

# who?

Kim Dae-jung

김대중

글 **이수정** | 그림 **스튜디오 청비** | 번역 **김성협** | 감수 **김수희**

Dasan Kid

Kim Dae-jung

Korean politician, January 6, 1924 ~ August 18, 2009

Kim Dae-jung is a politician who improved relations between the North and South on the divided Korean peninsula. He spent his childhood under the Japanese occupation of Korea, during which Koreans were not allowed to use their native language and could only study their nation's history in secret.

Kim learned about Korean history from his father and continued to gain more awareness of Korea's past. Korea was soon liberated from colonization but that victory was quickly followed by what is remembered to be the most tragic event in Korean history, the Korean war. It ended in a truce and resulted in a divided country. Kim Dae-jung witnessed the tragic war which was fought amongst fellow countrymen, and made the decision to become a politician.

After the division, Kim Dae-jung ran for office four times until he finally got elected. But just two days after the election, a dictatorship took over the government and he lost his position in the Parliament. However, Kim did not give up and became elected again to the Parliament. He did not succumb to the pressure of the dictatorship, fought for democratization, and finally became elected as the fifteenth President of Korea.

However, immediately after he became elected president, the nation faced a currency crisis. The government under Kim Dae-jung organized a gold collecting movement together with economic reform, and was able to recover from the crisis in a short time. Once the economy was stabilized, Kim poured his efforts into reconciling the stand-off between the North and South.

In order to improve the North-South relations, Kim Dae-jung introduced the Sunshine Policy. For the first time since the division, talks were held between the North and South. Other major exchanges with the North included reunions arranged between families separated by the war and a tourism business to visit Mount Keumkang in the North.

The politician who demonstrated unwavering courage under a dictatorship government and the president who improved relations between the two Koreas emphasizing reconciliation and cooperation, Kim Dae-jung later became the first Korean to receive the Nobel Peace Prize.

김대중

한국의 정치가, 1924년 1월 6일 ~ 2009년 8월 18일

분단 체제 안에서 남북 관계를 개선시킨 정치가 김대중은 일제 식민지 아래서 어린 시절을 보냈습니다. 일제의 지배 아래서 백성들은 우리말이 있어도 쓸 수 없었고 몰래 우리 역사를 배워야 했습니다.

김대중은 아버지의 가르침을 통해 우리나라의 역사를 배우고 역사 의식을 키워 나갔습니다. 해방이 되었지만 곧 한국사 최대의 비극으로 기억되는 6.25 전쟁이 났고 휴전되면서 우리나라는 분단국가가 되었습니다. 김대중은 같은 민족 사이에 벌어진 비극적인 전쟁을 보며 정치가가 되기로 결심합니다.

분단 이후 독재 정권이 장기화되면서 김대중은 네 번의 선거에서 패하고 당선된 지 이틀 만에 국회의원직을 박탈당하고 맙니다. 하지만 김대중은 포기하지 않고 도전해 국회의원에 당선됩니다. 독재 정권의 압박 아래서 굴하지 않고 민주화를 위해 노력했던 김대중은 마침내 제15대 대통령에 당선됩니다.

하지만 그가 대통령에 당선된 직후 우리나라는 외환위기를 맞게 됩니다. 김대중 정부는 국민들의 힘을 모아 '금 모으기 운동'과 경제 개혁으로 빠른 시일 안에 외환위기를 극복하게 됩니다. 경제 사정이 안정되자 김대중은 남북 문제에 힘을 쏟게 됩니다.

김대중은 남북 관계를 개선시키기 위해 햇볕 정책을 펼쳤습니다. 분단 이후 최초로 남북 정상 회담이 이루어졌고 이산가족 상봉과 금강산 관광 사업으로 남북 교류의 끈을 이어나갔습니다.

독재 정권 아래서 한결 같은 용기를 보여준 정치가 김대중은 대통령이 되어서는 화해와 협력에 바탕을 두고 남북 관계를 개선시킨 지도자로 인정받아 한국인으로는 최초로 노벨 평화상을 수상합니다.

이 책을 만든 사람들

글 · 이수정

우연히 접한 학습 만화의 매력에 푹 빠져서 어려운 내용을 어린이들의 눈높이에 맞게 쉽고 재미있게 설명할 수 있는 학습 만화 시나리오를 쓰게 되었습니다. 겉으로 보이는 위인들의 훌륭한 면뿐만 아니라 숨겨진 노력과 열정을 찾아내어 감동적인 이야기를 만들기 위해 노력합니다.

그림 · 스튜디오 청비

기발한 상상력을 바탕으로 새롭고 재미있는 콘텐츠를 만들어 내는 만화 창작 집단입니다. 어린이들이 책을 읽고 큰 꿈을 품기를 바라는 마음으로 즐겁게 작업하고 있습니다. 작품으로 『성철 스님』, 『아 다르고 어 다른 우리말 101가지』, 『반기문 유엔 사무총장의 꿈과 도전』 등이 있습니다.

번역 · 김성협(Sung H Kim)

한국에서 태어나 아프리카 케냐에서 자랐고 영국 런던에서 미술과 건축을 전공했습니다. 한국 콜럼버스 국제 유학원에서 부원장으로 일했으며 현대건설 국제 프로젝트 통역을 담당했습니다. 현재 〈디갤러리 서울〉과 〈더페이지 갤러리〉의 수석 큐레이터로 일하고 있습니다.

감수 · 김수희

연세대학교에서 역사를 전공했습니다. 이후 한국뿐 아니라 일본, 미국에서 한국어, 일본어, 영어를 가르쳐 왔으며 부모를 위한 영어교육용 책을 썼습니다. 영어교육채널 EBSe '엄마표 영어특강'에서 강의를 하며 홈스쿨, 알파벳과 파닉스, 다차원 테마 영어 수업 기법을 알리고 있습니다. 전국 각지에서 어린이 영어 교육에 대한 강연을 하며 창의적이고 열정적인 교수 법으로 영어를 배우고자 하는 어린이와 부모들에게 많은 도움을 주고 있습니다.

Kim Dae-jung

What prize was Kim Dae-jung awarded in 2000?

a. The Nobel Prize in Literature
b. The Nobel Prize in Physics
c. The Nobel Peace Prize

Answer: c

Contents

01 A Boy from the Island

Kim Dae-jung was born on January 6, 1924 in Jeonlanamdo Shinan-gun Haeu-myun, Haeu-do. Haeu-do is a beautiful island located southwest of the South Korean Peninsula. Haeu means a dress made of lotus flowers because the shape of the island is similar to a full bloomed lotus flower.

Wow! That must be a Japanese warship! It is so large!
Why doesn't Korea have such amazing warships?
We could be free from Japanese colonization if we had warships like that...

11

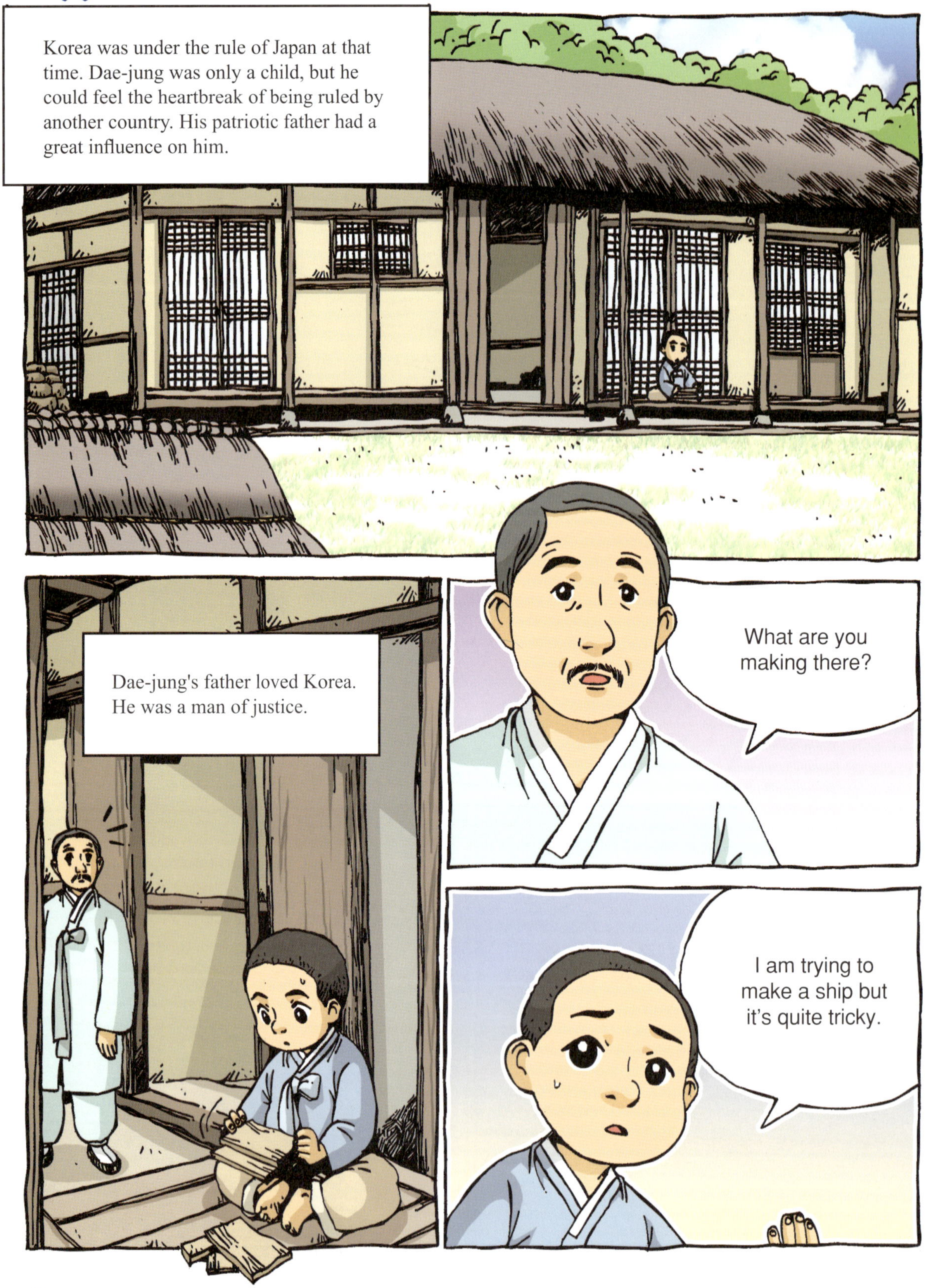

Korea was under the rule of Japan at that time. Dae-jung was only a child, but he could feel the heartbreak of being ruled by another country. His patriotic father had a great influence on him.

Dae-jung's father loved Korea. He was a man of justice.

What kind of ship is this?
It looks strange.
It is a large warship.
A warship, is it?
Shall we make it together?
Yes!
Unlike other fathers, Dae-jung's father was not authoritative, nor patriarchal. Instead, he was kind and loving and often made toys with Dae-jung.
It is done now!
Let's go and see if it floats.

Father! Look! It floats.
Of course it floats. Hahaha!
Oh, are you back from town already?
Oh my, I forgot.
What do you mean, you forgot?
I was on my way but Dae-jung was making a ship and I...

*Princess Jung Myeong: First daughter of SeonJo,
the 14th King of Chosun Dynasty.
*tenant farmer: Farmers who live on borrowed land.

Track 04

Dae-jung grew up watching his father fighting against injustice.

I am going to be a strong and just man like my father.

Rotten people! They arrested an innocent person and beat him badly!

What happened to him? Was he released?

It seems like he won't be released that easy this time.

Oh my... How awful...

*Chosun Dynasty Genealogy: Records of Korean kings names and their achievements.
*Chosun: An empire which later became the Republic of Korea.

One day, a merchant visited the island.

Although it was forbidden to teach Korean history, Dae-jung's father still taught him the history of the Chosun Dynasty.

Look! It is a traveling merchant!

Travelling merchants at that time sold items like candies, combs, cosmetics, and mirrors. Children were always amazed at all the things they could not usually see on the island.
Let's take a look at his stuff.
Okay.
Hey, look at this, isn't it cool?
Wow!
ZZZ...
ZZZ! ZZZ!

What are you doing?!
Hey, it's okay. This guy wouldn't know if a few things are missing from his stuff. You guys should take a few things too. Hurry!
Unfortunately, the children took a few things from the merchant.
This is stealing. Stealing is bad...
Dae-jung was scared. He knew it was a bad thing to do. But he could not stop the children.

What are you waiting for? You should take one as well.
No, I'm not going to.
You are going to miss out! It is your loss.

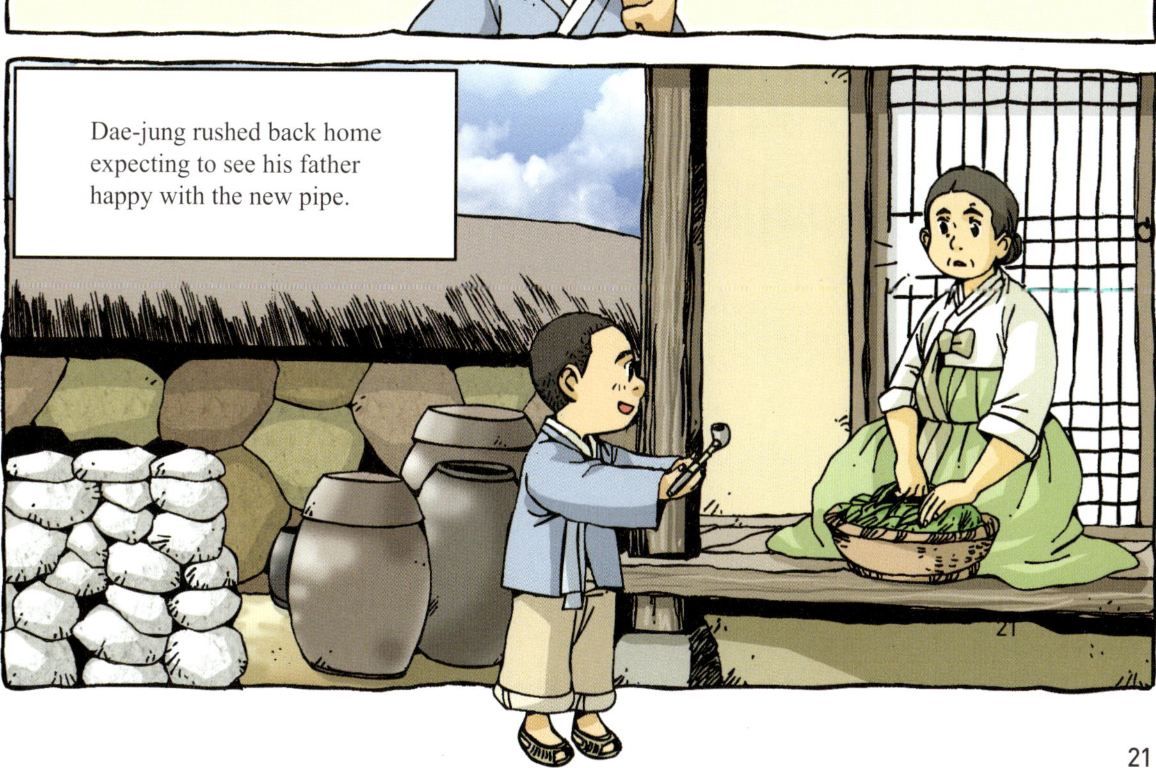

Dae-jung suddenly remembered his father's worn-out smoking pipe. He could no longer think clearly.
Yeah... Father's pipe is too old and worn out. He will be happy if I bring this to him.
Dae-jung rushed back home expecting to see his father happy with the new pipe.

Dae-jung never saw his mother that upset before. Frightened, he told her the truth.

Although his mother loved him very much, she could not overlook wrongful deeds and so she punished him.
SLAP
SLAP
I'm sorry, Mother. I will never steal ever again.
SLAP
Lead the way.
Yes, Mother.

Track 08

She went to see the merchant with Dae-jung.

Excuse me, wake up!

Wh-what's wrong?

I came to return something my child stole.

What are you doing? You give him back the pipe now.

I am so sorry, sir.
Forgive me please. Sob sob...
She asked for forgiveness and explained what had happened. Dae-jung was so ashamed he could not look up.
It is the children's fault for sure. But you tempted the children by leaving your items in the open like that. Please be careful not to make the same mistake again.
Um...

My my, to be lectured at my age... but then, that lady is right after all.

Dae-jung deeply regretted stealing.

So, are you thinking that it is not fair? Because you didn't start it but you got punished for it?

I am sorry, Mother. All my friends were doing it and I...

No, Mother.
Sob sob...
Listen, you should have stopped your friends when they were about to do bad things. It is worse when you ignore injustice. You need so much courage and patience to be an honest man.
From this day on, Dae-jung always worked hard to follow the right path.

Fighting for Justice

When Dae-jung turned seven, he began to study at Seodang*. There was no public school on the island at that time, so children of the island studied at Seodang.

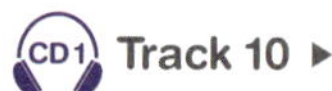

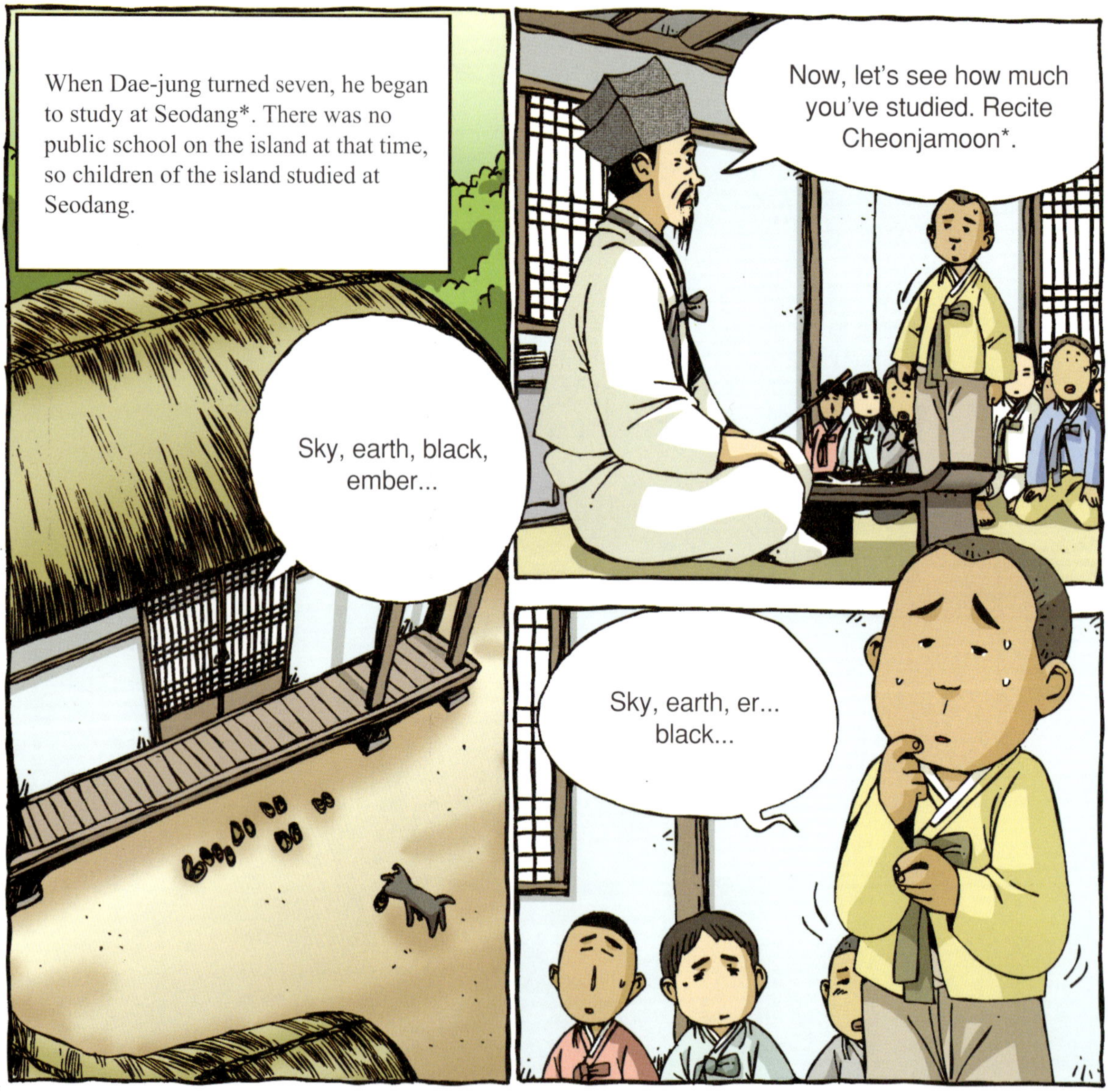

*Seodang: A traditional village school of Korea.
*Cheonjamoon: The Thousand Classic Characters.

Is that all you have memorized?
Next, you try to recite.

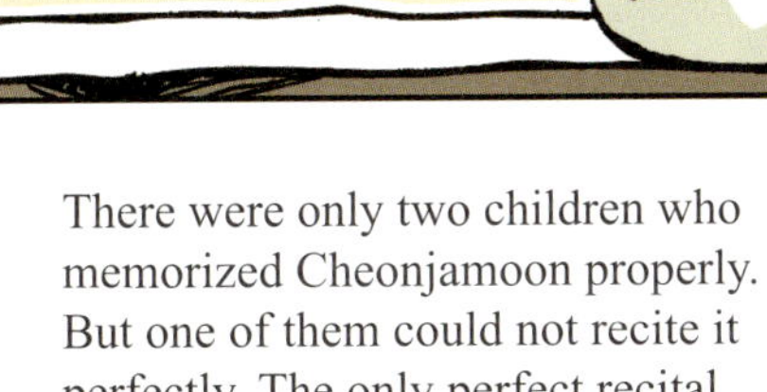
All the children at Seodang were tested on Cheonjamoon.

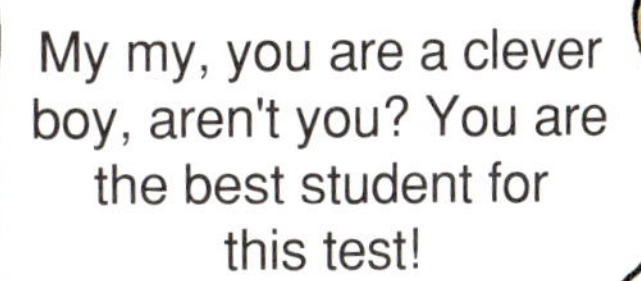
There were only two children who memorized Cheonjamoon properly. But one of them could not recite it perfectly. The only perfect recital was done by Dae-jung.

My my, you are a clever boy, aren't you? You are the best student for this test!
Wow!
CLAP CLAP

Dae-jung had a very good memory. He memorized all the things that he read or saw. He was always praised by the teacher.
Mother! Father!
What is it? Calm down.
What's all the excitement about?
Listen, I was the best student at a test today!
Oh my! Are you serious? My son is the best student?

Yes, Mother!
His parents were very happy to hear this news. His mother was especially excited because education was very important to her.
My son, you must study hard. I will do everything I can to get you thoroughly educated.
Yes, Mother.

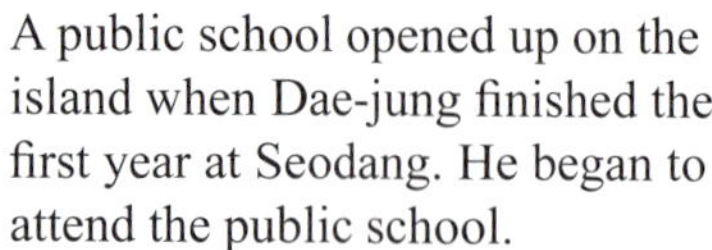

A public school opened up on the island when Dae-jung finished the first year at Seodang. He began to attend the public school.

But the public school only had a four year course. He would have to move to the city if he wanted to study further, so his parents decided to move to Mokpo for higher education.

His parents opened a small inn to pay for his education. Dae-jung never disappointed his parents and always got the highest score in his tests.

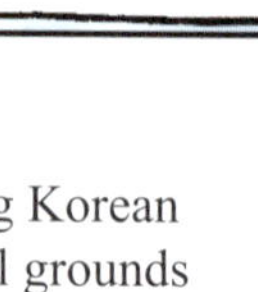

By the time Dae-jung entered the sixth grade, the Japanese had banned the Korean language lessons.

Anyone speaking Korean within the school grounds would be punished.

How can this be? Koreans are not allowed to speak Korean...
One day his father came to visit him at the school.
Hmm...
Ah...

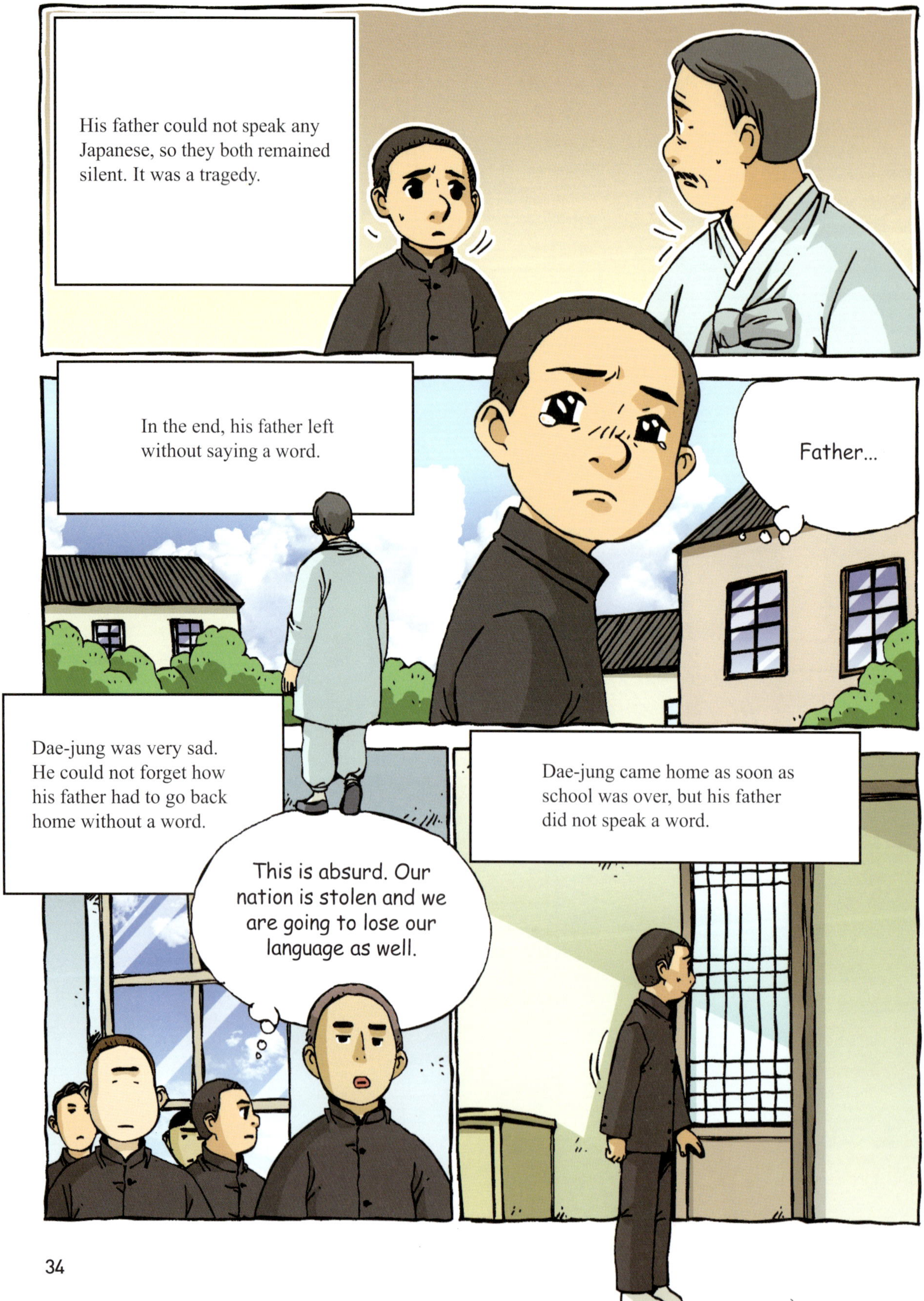

His father could not speak any Japanese, so they both remained silent. It was a tragedy.

In the end, his father left without saying a word.

Dae-jung was very sad. He could not forget how his father had to go back home without a word.

Dae-jung came home as soon as school was over, but his father did not speak a word.

After one year, Dae-jung graduated at the top of his class and was accepted into one of the most prestigious schools in Korea, Mokpo Business Public School.

The townspeople were very proud of him. His parents were happy that Dae-jung had achieved so much from his limited environment.

You must be happy.

It is nothing really.

What do you mean it is nothing? He was ahead of all the Japanese students. It is more than amazing. We are all so proud of him.

Dae-jung was always at the top of the class even in his new school. He studied hard to get better results than the Japanese students.

Hey Dae-jung, let's go already.

Go where?

It is time for today's lecture.

I will read a bit more and go. You go first.

I think he studies way too much.

Mokpo Business Public School Lecture
We must work hard and support Japan.
CLAP
CLAP CLAP
Wait, I have a question!
That's all for today's lecture.

*Josenjing: Japanese slang used during the colonization period. It is a very offensive word to describe Koreans.

The lecturer was embarrassed by Dae-jung's question. All the Japanese teachers and students began to dislike him.

But I...

Kim Dae-jung! How dare you ask such a question during the lecture! Are you insane? I will not tolerate such attitude ever again! Do you understand?

Will you disobey me again? Tell me!

No, I wont!

I will keep an eye on you! Now go!

Are you okay?

Yes, sir.

I know you are a bright student. But you really need to be careful. It wouldn't be good for you if you are against them.

Dae-jung was class president for three years. But his strong leadership sometimes caused troubles.

Are you ordering me?
You are only a Josenjing. It is funny how you became class president.
I didn't force you to accept me. And I became class president with a fair election.
Whatever!
You stink of Josenjing! Get out of the way!
Apologize!
Why should I? I said that you stink because you do stink like Josenjing.
You should present a proper argument if you have problems!
...

Track 17
Take this!
Dae-jung lost control and punched the Japanese student. This fight developed into a big fight between Japanese and Korean students.
What is this nonsense!? Stop it right now!

School life became more difficult for Dae-jung after the fight. Senior Japanese students began to bully Dae-jung almost every day.
I will never submit to Japanese rule! Never!
He began to get lower grades at the school after he handed in an essay strongly criticizing Japanese colonization.
Japanese teachers didn't give him a good grade even when he studied really hard. It was because Dae-jung was always speaking against the Japanese colonization of Korea. He gave up being a class president and studied hard to get into university.

43

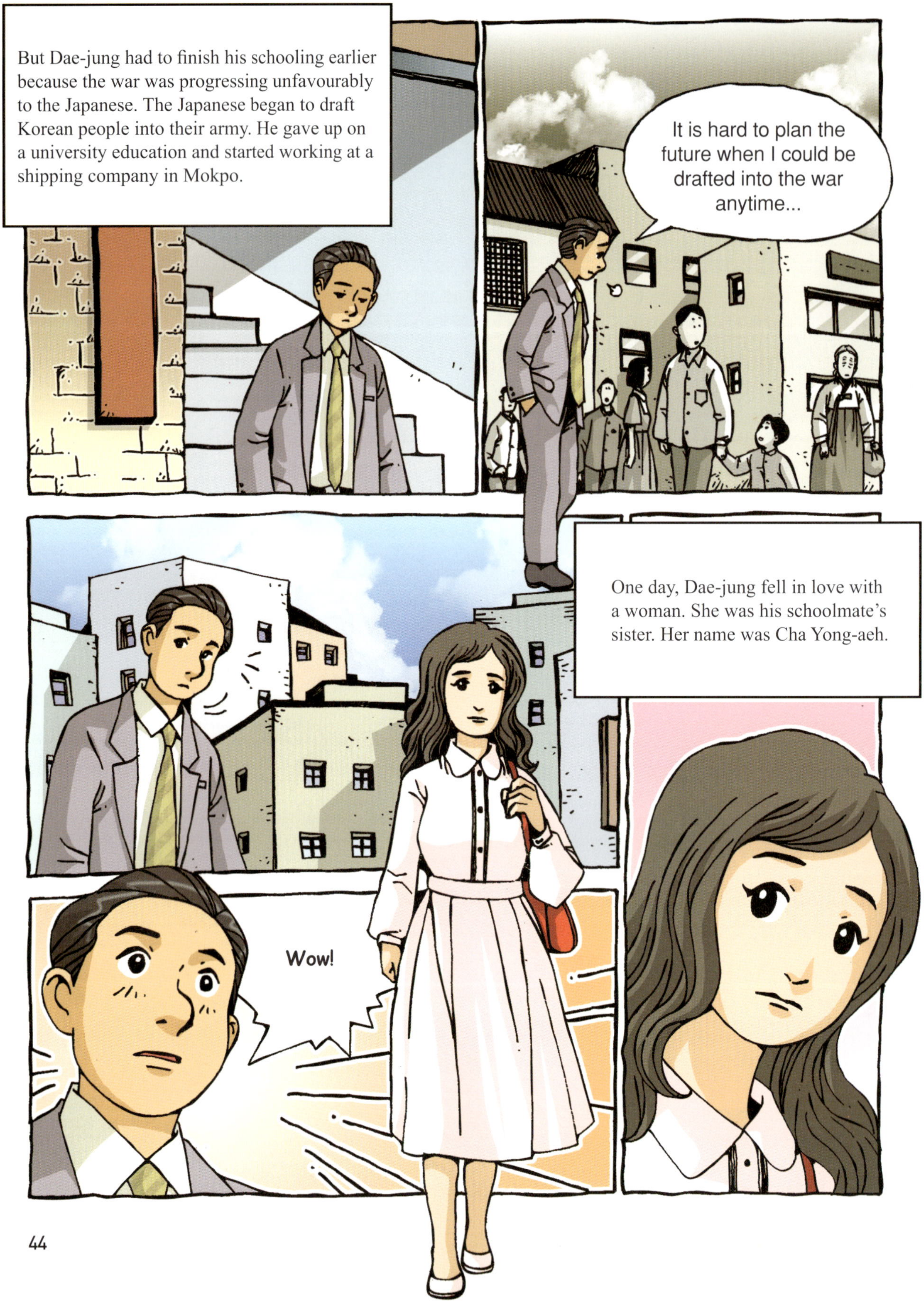

But Dae-jung had to finish his schooling earlier because the war was progressing unfavourably to the Japanese. The Japanese began to draft Korean people into their army. He gave up on a university education and started working at a shipping company in Mokpo.

One day, Dae-jung fell in love with a woman. She was his schoolmate's sister. Her name was Cha Yong-aeh.

She finally agreed to marry him after Dae-jung persevered in proposing to her. They wedded in April 1945. Although their honeymoon began happily, Dae-jung was unsure of when the Japanese would draft him away from his happy life.

A few months passed. Korea finally became independent when the King of Japan unconditionally surrendered on May 15, 1945.

The war is finally over!

When the war was finished and Korea became independent, the shipping company owner, who was Japanese, left the company to Dae-jung.

Please take good care of the company. You are the one I trusted the most.

I will make this company big and it will help Chosun become stronger.

*National Establishment Committee: A government body that was in charge of stabilizing the nation after the independence.

03 Stepping into Politics

Dae-jung was becoming a well- known business man in Korea. He contracted many ships and companies to expand his business.

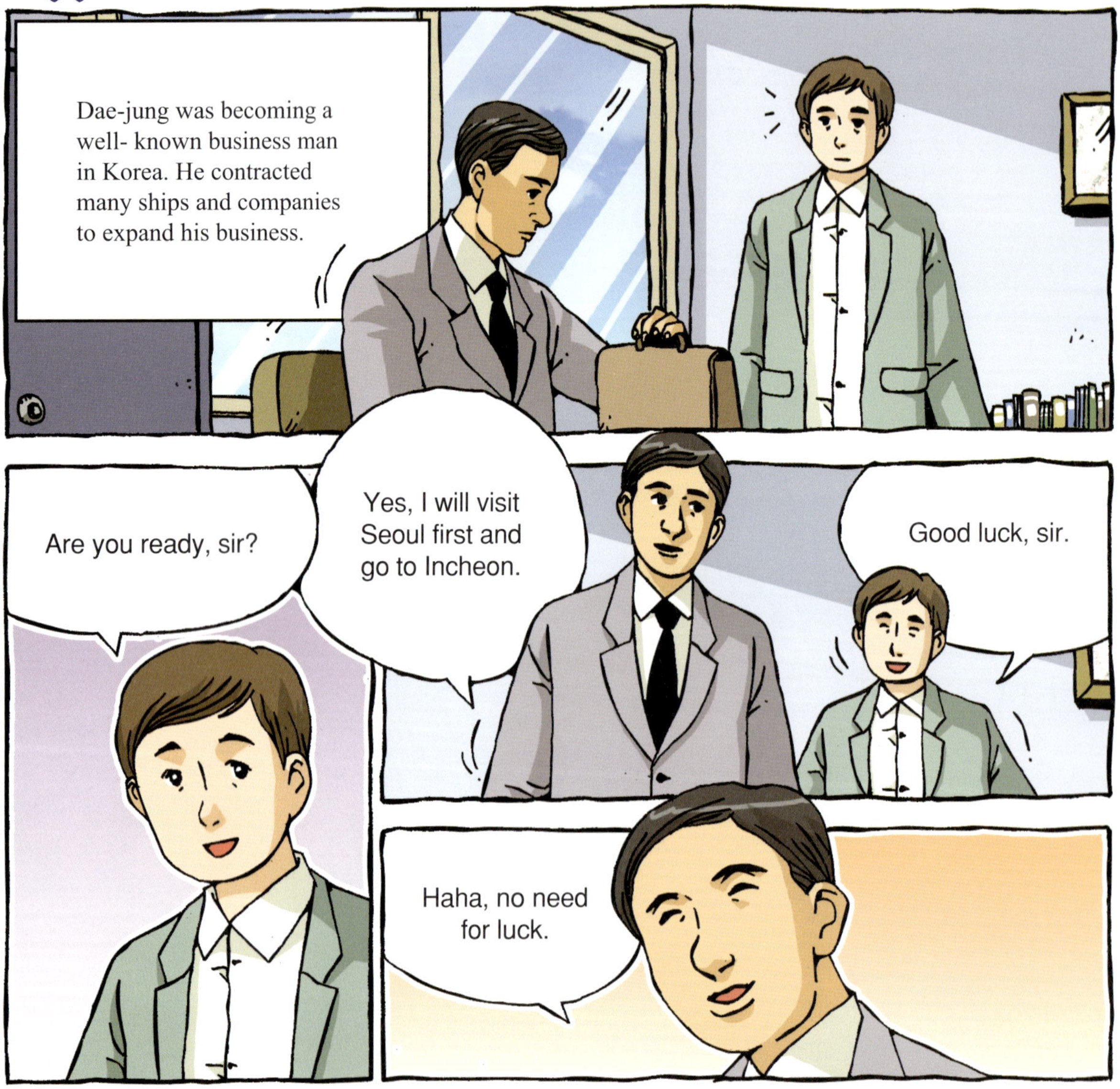

It was about ten days since he had arrived in Seoul for business. While walking down the street with his military friend, Dae-jung heard terrible news.
All military personnel should return to the base immediately!
What is happening?
I have no idea. I will have to return to the base anyway.
I have to know what is happening.

Northern commies declared a war.
It was June 25, 1950—four days after North Korea had declared war. President Rhee Syng-man of South Korea tried to calm the people down through the radio.
We will protect Seoul with whatever it takes. Citizens do not need to panic.

*Gwanghwamun: A palace gate located in the center of Seoul.

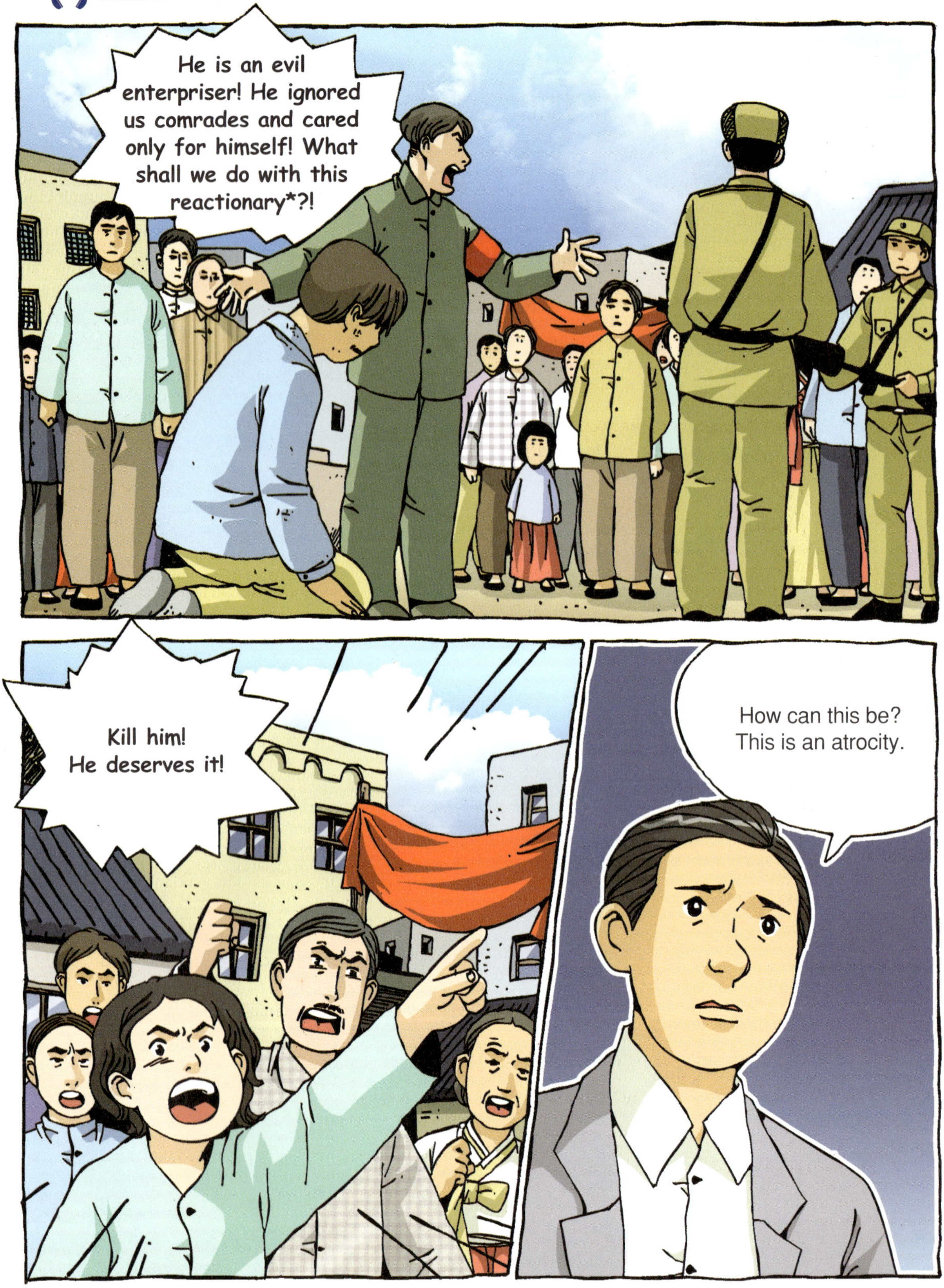

*reactionary: A reactionary person or group tries to prevent changes in the political or social system of their country.

They are going to kill us all. What is the South Korean army doing?

They are busy saving the 'important people.' The president ran away before he even tried to protect Seoul. I don't think they care for powerless commoners like us anyway.

This kind of tragedy should never happen again.

Dae-jung barely managed to reach Mokpo. He went through many near-death experiences on the way.

Oh thank goodness, you are alive.

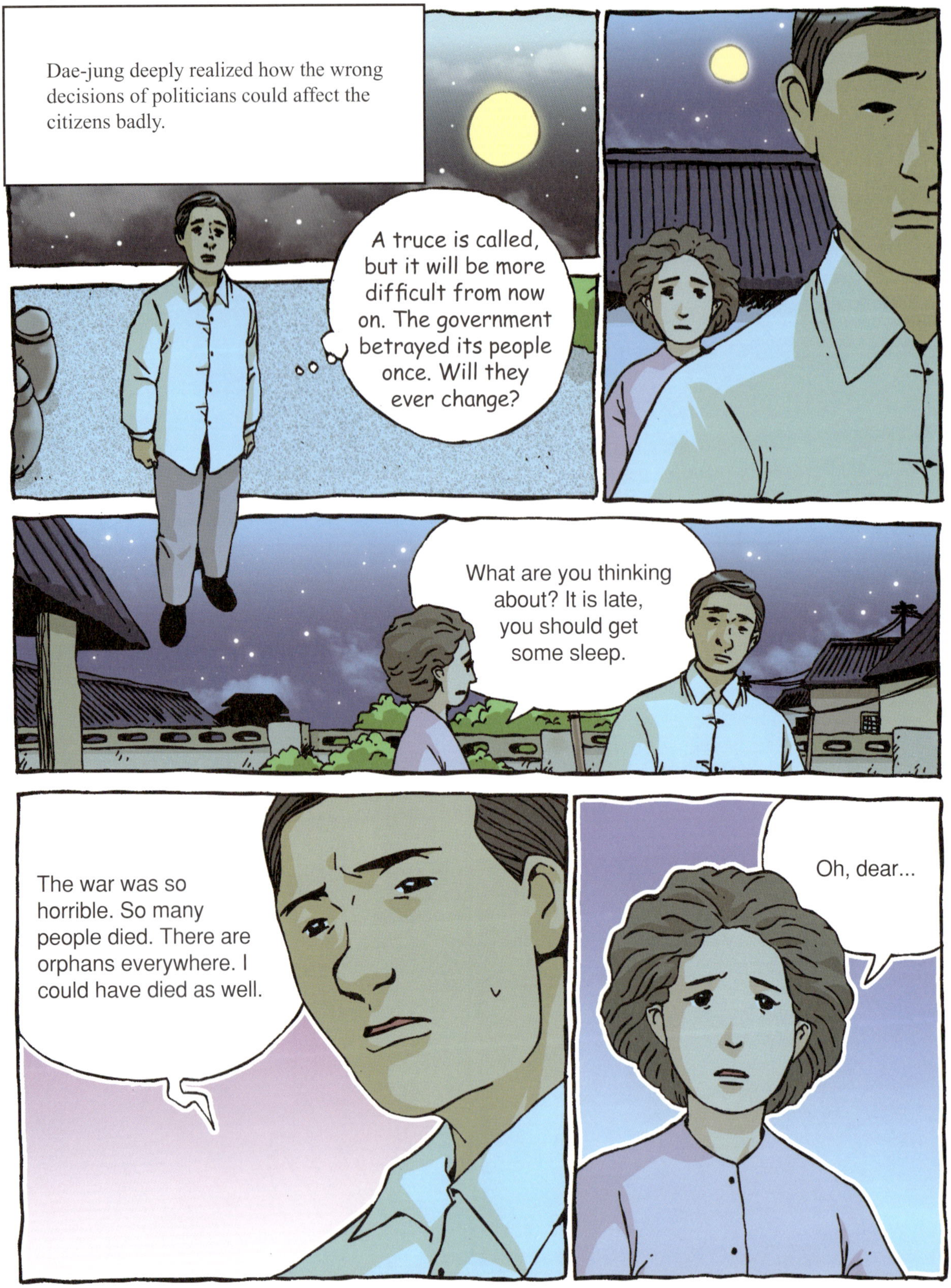

Dae-jung deeply realized how the wrong decisions of politicians could affect the citizens badly.

This would not have happened if there was a righteous leader. All the politicians were corrupt and selfish. We have been sacrificed for their greed.
I made up my mind. I will sacrifice myself for the nation. I don't want people to suffer from rotten politicians anymore.
Would you support me?
Of course.
It won't be easy. But if we give up because it is difficult, we won't achieve anything.
I am always on your side. I will support you whatever you do.
Thank you so much.

*House of Representatives: 1960~1961. It was elected by citizens.

*Freedom Party: A conservative party of Korea. It was founded in Busan in December 1951 with Rhee Syng-man as a representative. It became a dictating party after it became a ruling party of Korean government. The party committed fraudulent election in 1960 and was overthrown after 4.19 Revolution.

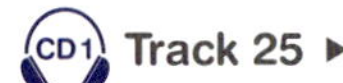

The dictatorship of President Rhee Syng-man threatened people who supported other parties. Such outrageous things were happening all around the nation at that time.
See? It would have been much easier if you gave in earlier.
Labor Union members were threatened to support the Freedom Party. Dae-jung lost the election in the end.
We are sorry, they threatened us badly...
No, don't worry about me for now. Take care of yourself first.
The tyranny of the Freedom Party and President Rhee Syng-man continued until it was overthrown.

*national convention: A nationwide assembly held by a political party.

But Dae-jung could not even be registered as a candidate because the Freedom Party had interfered with every process of the election.

Dear!

I am so sorry... I have not been the best father or best husband... I have used all of our money because of all the politics. I just don't know what to do.

What are you talking about? This is not like you at all. You must fight for justice.

Dae-jung was glad that his wife fully supported him instead of complaining.

Thank you so much, dear.

Fortunately, the fraudulent election of the Freedom Party was exposed and the election result became invalid. The election was reheld. This time, Dae-jung became one of the candidates.
But the Freedom Party was still corrupt. They placed high ranking officers at polling stations to check every soldier's election paper.
Outrageous!
The Freedom Party worked so hard for the nation! And you dare vote for Kim Dae-jung?
Give it to me!
Okay, go now.

Track 27

Dae-jung lost the election again.
But his tragedy did not end there.

Dear!

Are you awake?

D-dear,
I am so
sorry...

What do you
mean? You only
need to think
about getting
better!

You should never give up. Achieve your dream.
Your dream is my dream as well.
His wife had died. She had always supported him and never complained even after moving homes several times for Dae-jung's political dreams. It was a tragic loss for Dae-jung.
Dear! No!

04 Enduring Hardships

President Rhee Syng-man's corrupt dictatorship* continued and grew worse each day. There was no freedom of speech and people were arrested without reason. On April 19, 1960, after Rhee Syng-man had been fraudulently re-elected again, the citizens were no longer patient and began to riot.

That day, thousands of people were injured and 183 people died in Seoul. Dae-jung fought with them. The nationwide demonstration could not be kept under control. 12 years of dictatorship finally ended. It was a victory for democracy in which many people were sacrificed. This incident is called the 4.19 Revolution.

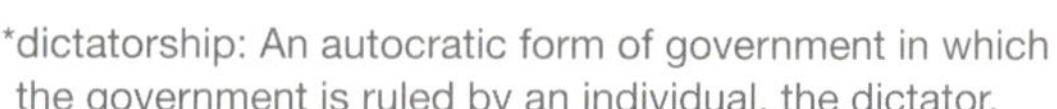

*dictatorship: An autocratic form of government in which the government is ruled by an individual, the dictator.

Jang Myun became prime minister of the new government. He appointed Dae-jung as a spokesperson and the planning committee head of the Democratic Party. It was the first time that a non-congress member had been appointed to this position.

There must be a better person. Can't you reconsider?

No, I believe that you are the right person for the job. You make excellent speeches. You should be the spokesperson. Also, I don't know anyone who has stronger beliefs than you do. Believe in yourself.

I will do my best.

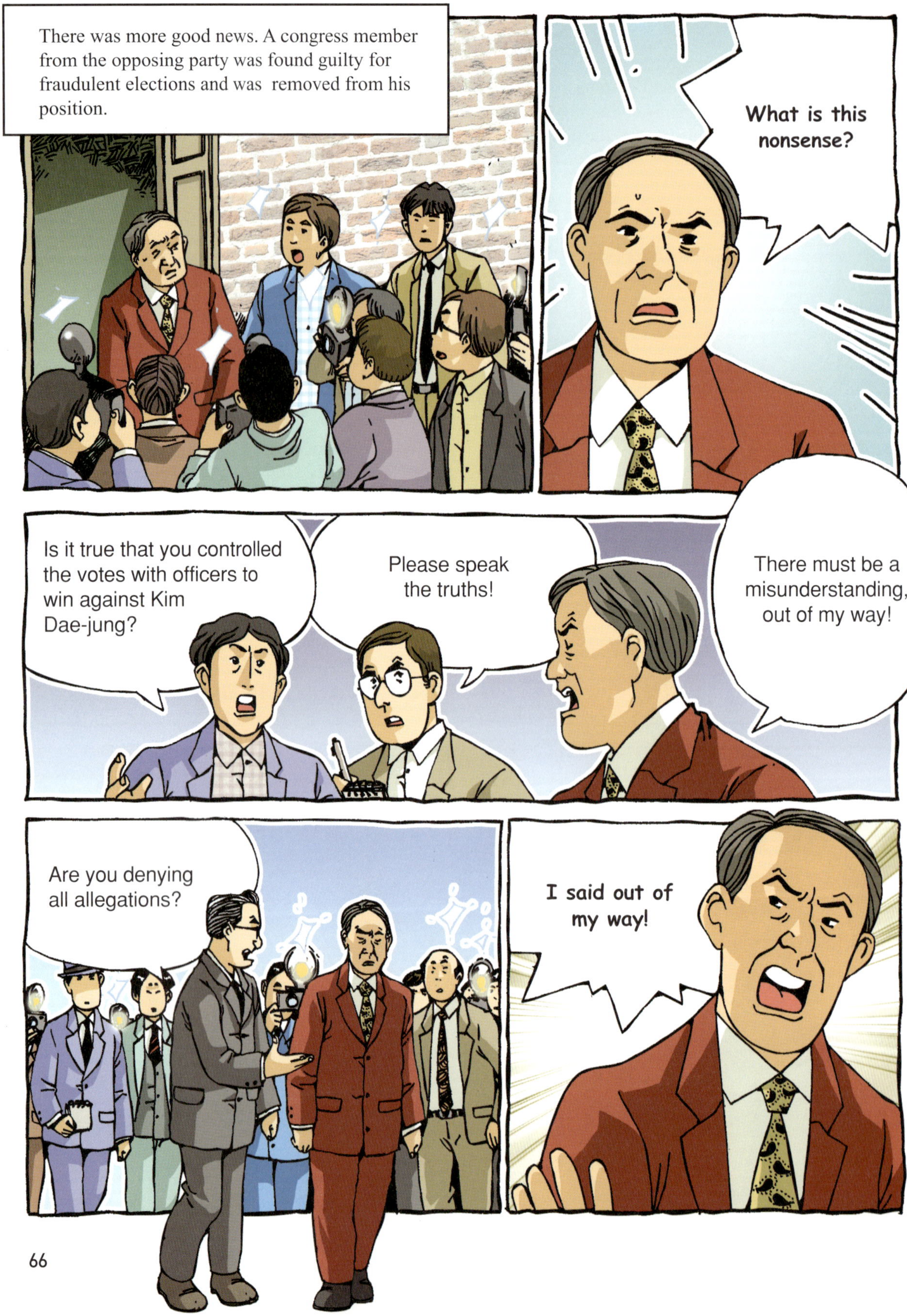

There was more good news. A congress member from the opposing party was found guilty for fraudulent elections and was removed from his position.
What is this nonsense?
Is it true that you controlled the votes with officers to win against Kim Dae-jung?
Please speak the truths!
There must be a misunderstanding, out of my way!
Are you denying all allegations?
I said out of my way!

Dae-jung finally got elected as a lower house representative of Gangwon province, Inje region on May 14, 1961. It was seven years since he had stepped into politics.
Congratulations, sir.
No, I should thank you for voting for me. I am grateful for your support.
Please lead the nation with clean politics. We expect so much from you.
I will never forget your support.
Hurray! Kim Dae-jung!

Dae-jung promised that he would do his very best to show them clean politics.

I am what I am because these people believe in me.

But Dae-jung couldn't be a congressman for long.

RING RING

Who is calling me at this time?

*coup: An illegal way of taking over ruling power with military force.

Park Jung-hee and his followers justified themselves by declaring that they would clear out all corruption and incompetent politicians. They began to occupy major facilities of Korea.

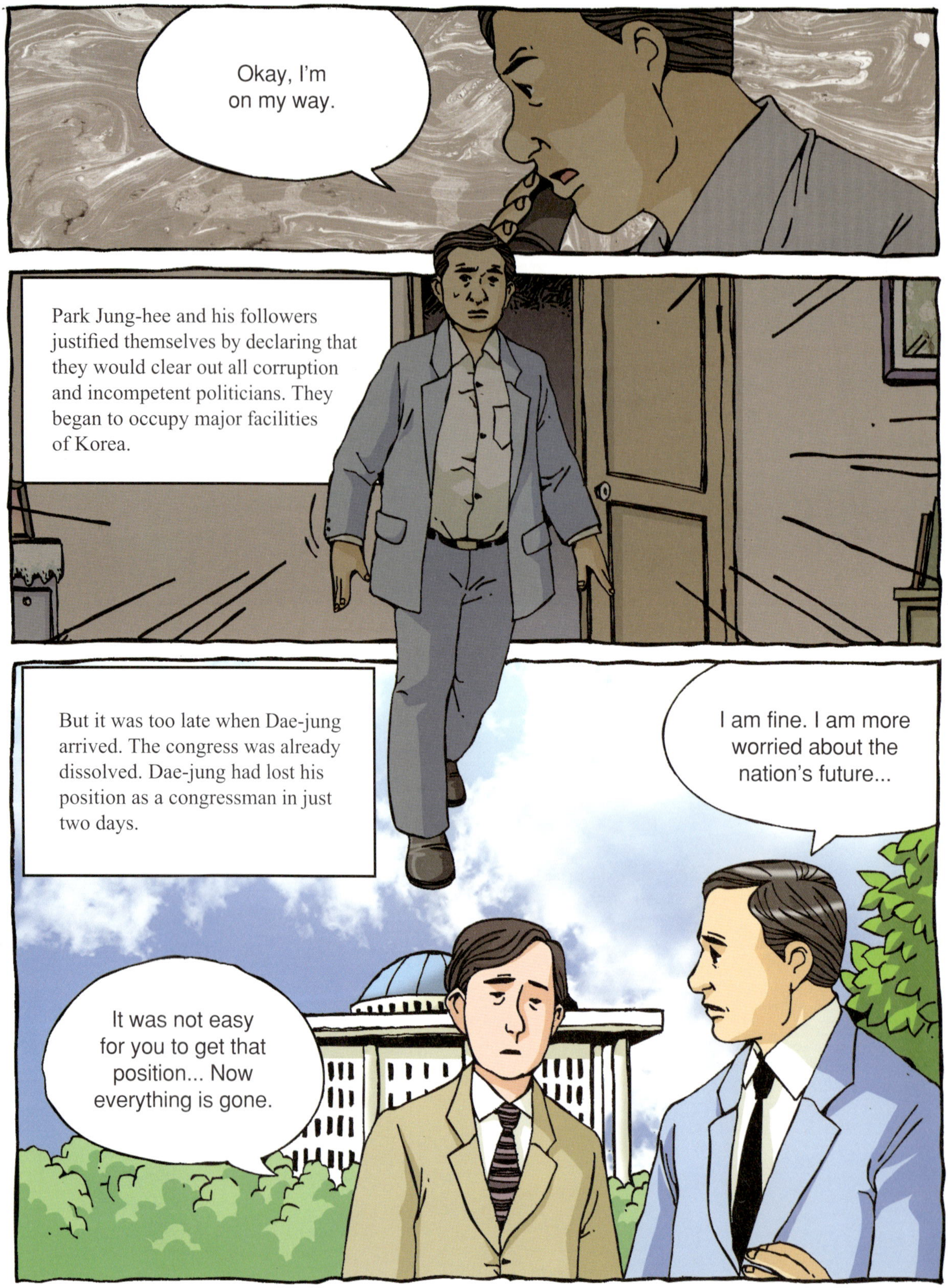

But it was too late when Dae-jung arrived. The congress was already dissolved. Dae-jung had lost his position as a congressman in just two days.

*embezzlement: Crime of using someone else's money.

Now, explain how you embezzled public assets while you were a spokesperson of the Democratic Party.
Nonsense! I did no such thing!
You helped commies during the war, didn't you?
I never did such thing.
I am sure we can find some record! It will be easier if you just told me.
Find it if you can. You will only find that I am an innocent man.

Why don't you admit your crimes?
They tried to accuse Dae-jung of crimes he hadn't commited. But Dae-jung did not surrender.
I have never committed any crimes that I can admit.
Wait and see, we will find something.
Go ahead and try.

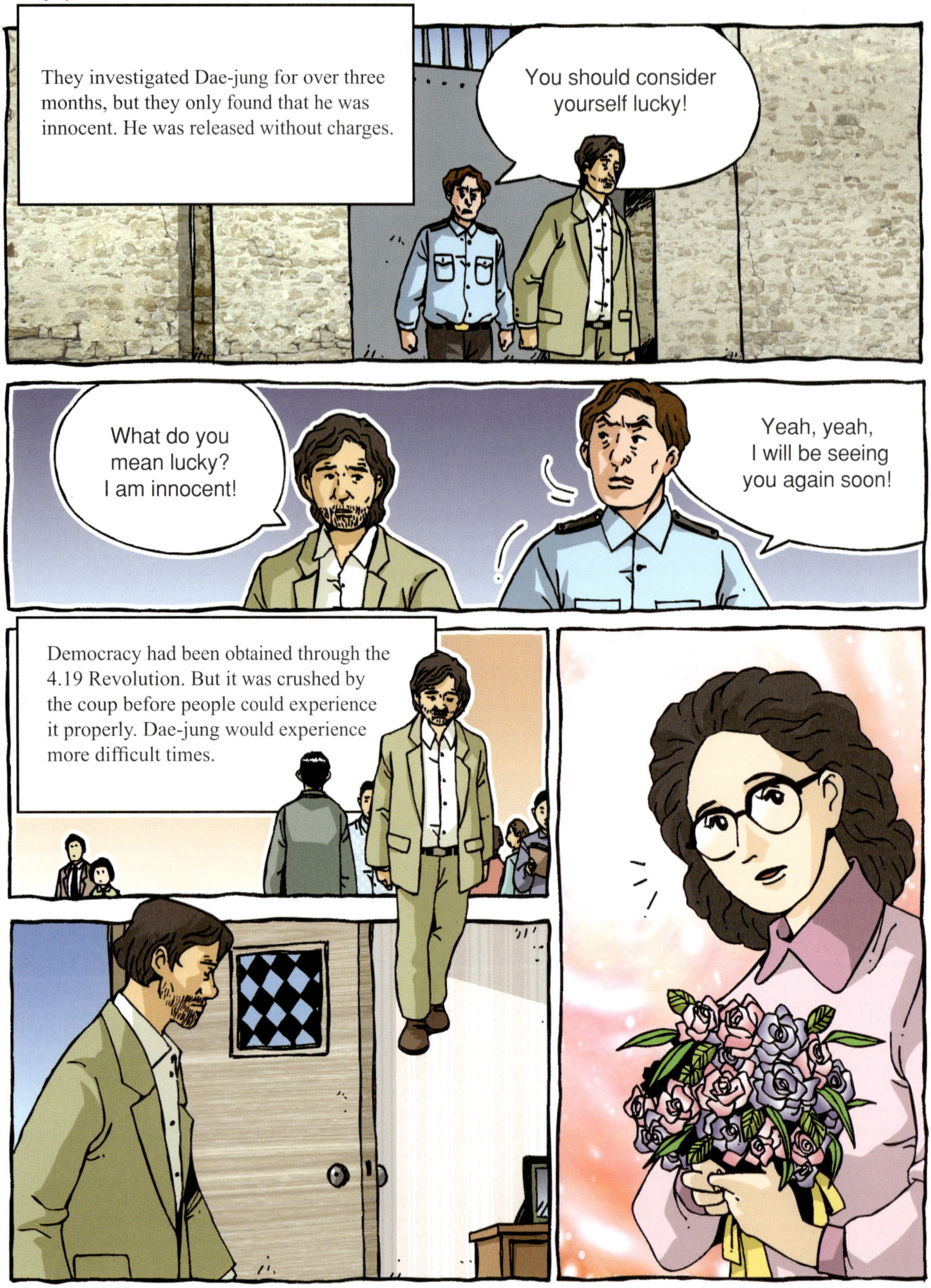

They investigated Dae-jung for over three months, but they only found that he was innocent. He was released without charges.

Democracy had been obtained through the 4.19 Revolution. But it was crushed by the coup before people could experience it properly. Dae-jung would experience more difficult times.

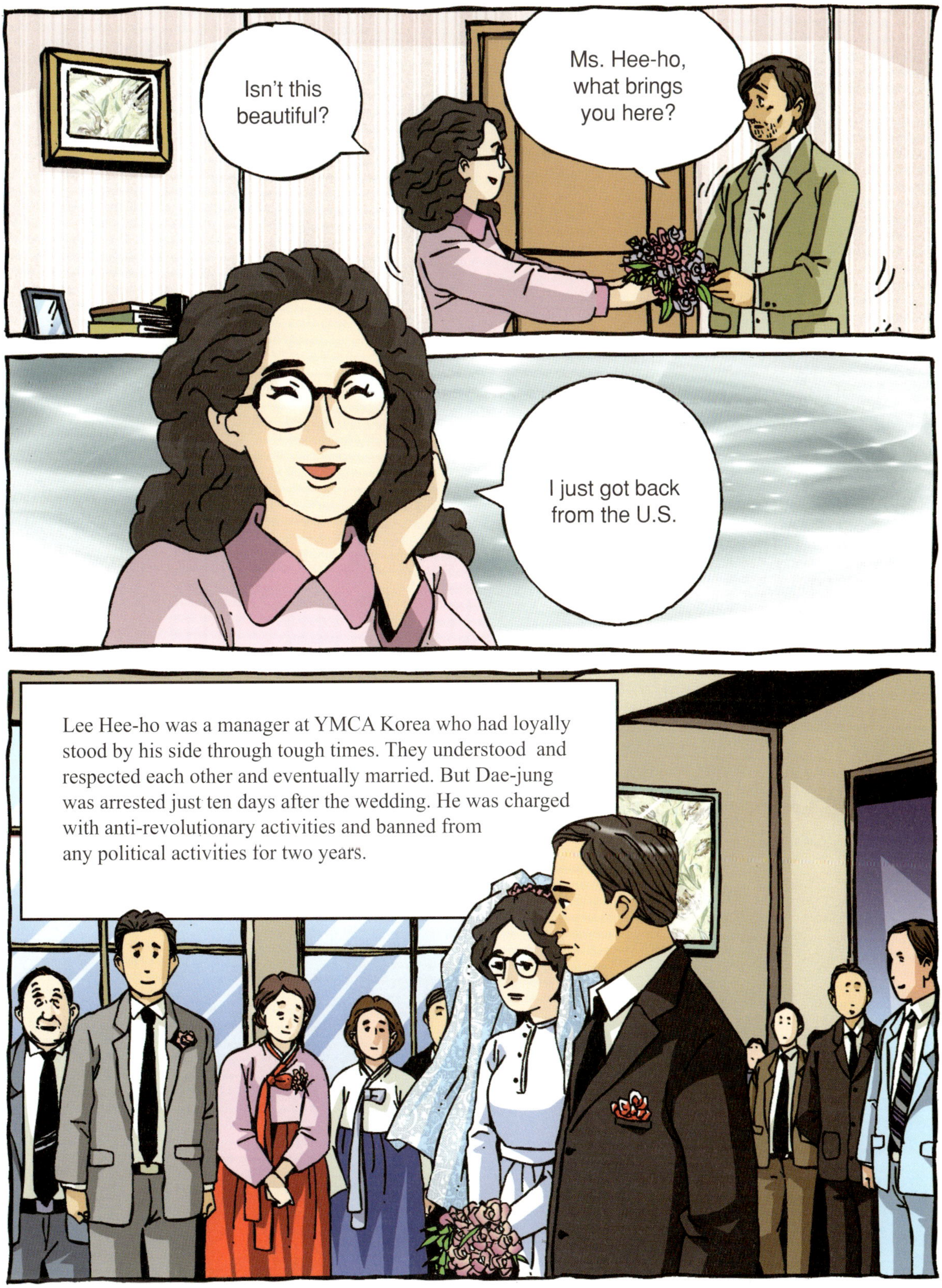

Lee Hee-ho was a manager at YMCA Korea who had loyally stood by his side through tough times. They understood and respected each other and eventually married. But Dae-jung was arrested just ten days after the wedding. He was charged with anti-revolutionary activities and banned from any political activities for two years.

Kim Dae-jung!

In 1963, the ban was lifted so Dae-jung returned to Mokpo to run for elections. Mokpo citizens greeted his return by officially electing him a congressman.

Congratulations! It is your first step into the congress. I knew you could do it.

I will do my best for justice and the people.

After so many obstacles, Dae-jung finally fulfilled his dream of being a congressman. He went to the National Assembly Library every single day to research national policies. When the library was closed, he brought the entire research data home to continue studying.

In 1964, he made a speech in the National Assembly. He argued about the unjust imprisonment of a congress member for 5 hours. The congress member was not arrested in the end and the speech was recognized by the Guinness Book of World Records as the longest speech ever made.

He always practiced speeches when he was the spokesperson for the Democratic Party. The public began to call him Dae-jung of great speech.

The 7th national election of Korea was held in June 1967.
The 1967 elections were as dangerous as ever with the military
regime suppressing the press and basic freedoms of expression.
Under this reign of terror, many politicians shifted their
attitude or gave up.

But Dae-jung ran for election in Mokpo
again, all the while bravely criticizing
the military in public speeches.

This nation does not belong to
a military regime! This nation
should be ruled by citizens!

Kim Dae-jung

Kim

The military regime said that they took over the government to clear out corruption! But the military regime of Park Jung-hee is more corrupt than ever!

That's right!

You see? It seems the only person who can fight against Park Jung-hee is Kim Dae-jung.

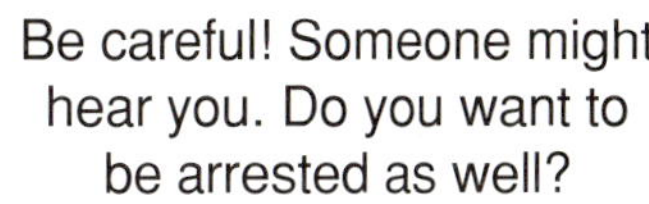

Be careful! Someone might hear you. Do you want to be arrested as well?

Citizens loved Dae-jung for his honesty and bravery. They hoped for true democracy and supported Dae-jung, reelecting him as congressman once more.
Kim Dae-jung!
Kim Dae-jung!

 CD 2 **Track 01** ▶

In 1970, Park Jung-hee tried to become president again by changing the constitution. Dae-jung criticized him for becoming a dictator.

With the support of the people, Dae-jung became a presidential election candidate. He was only 47. The people hoped that Kim Dae-jung could bring true democracy to Korea.

Large crowds gathered wherever he made his speeches. It showed how much people wanted democracy.

Dae-jung's great speeches and his brave convictions were enough to win people's hearts.

Even the foreign press media reported his potential to overthrow the military regime.

To deter people from attending Dae-jung's speeches, the military regime forced public workers to work on Sundays, called for emergency training and even opened movie theaters for free.

But on April 18, 1971, Janchungdan Park was packed with more than a million people who had gathered to hear his speech. Considering that the population of Seoul was four million at that time, it was a remarkable number. It was recorded as one of the greatest election campaigns of world history.

Let's get rid of corruption!
Dictatorship is wrong!
My fellow citizens! Park Jung-hee destroyed democracy with a military coup!
What's more? He is going to change the constitution to become a president again! What do we need to do?
Get rid of the military regime! Fair and clean election!
Let us show him the power of the people!
Let us make him realize what true democracy really is!

People cheered at his speech against dictatorship.
That's right!
Kim Dae-jung!
Our next president!
Unlike the military regime which recognized North Korea as a threatening enemy state, Dae-jung tried to encourage the idea of peaceful unification.
But Korea is meant to be one nation! What do we need in this divided nation?
The military regime is trying to create a society filled with fear! They say that North Korea is an enemy state!
We need communication and respect! We need peaceful unification!
We need to exchange our culture and sports events. We need to communicate! We need to achieve unification peacefully!

Because Koreans were not even allowed to sing *Our Wish is Unification* at that time his speech was very controversial. His idea of unification was supported only by students and a few scholars but the military regime accused him of being a communist.

There was corruption in ballot counting as well. 2,700 votes became invalid at Dae-jung's hometown. They said that the voting stamp was invalid.

When the voting began, the military regime tried all kinds of corrupt tactics to win the votes. They replaced ballots with fake votes and even entered votes under the names of deceased people.

Park Jung-hee became the president once again. Analysts said that Dae-jung would have won the election by one million votes if there was no corruption involved.

Don't feel too bad, sir. They were only 970 thousand votes ahead of us, even with all the illegal activities.

It's like you won this election in a way.

I am not disappointed. There are five million people who support me. That is enough for now.

The 8th national congress elections began right after the presidential election. Dae-jung traveled around the nation asking for the support of the people for his party members.

Park Jung-hee is aiming for a permanent regime! Give us votes! Let's not give him the power to change the constitution as he wants!

The congress member elections was as heated as the presidential election. Many Democratic Party candidates asked Dae-jung to make speeches for them.

Wh-what?
CRASH
Are you okay, sir?
I-I think
I am okay.
Are you okay?

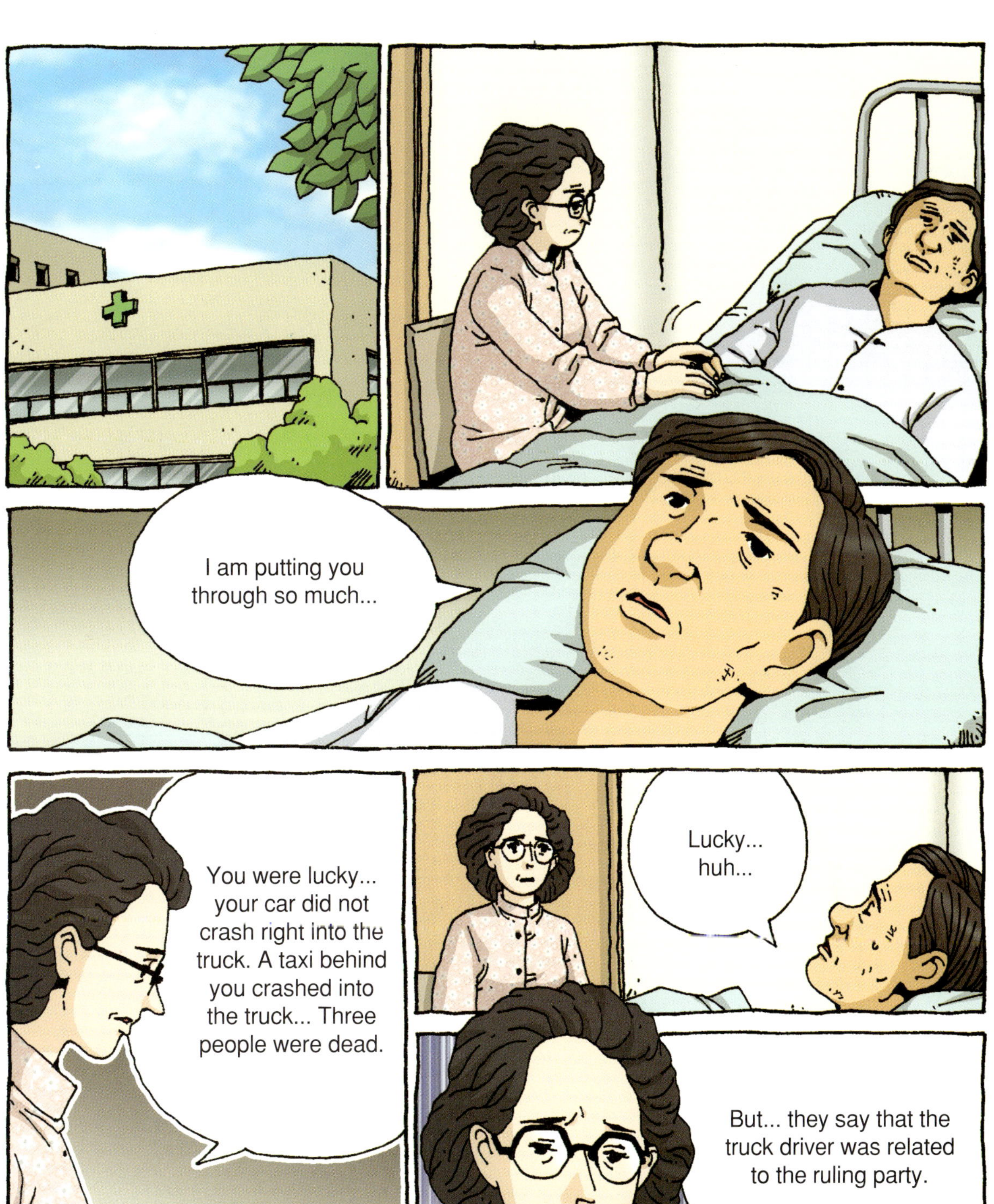

I am putting you through so much...
You were lucky... your car did not crash right into the truck. A taxi behind you crashed into the truck... Three people were dead.
Lucky... huh...
But... they say that the truck driver was related to the ruling party.

The court ruled the case as a simple accident and the media did not report the accident at all. The people never realized that this had happened and Dae-jung was no longer able to walk properly.

While Dae-jung was in Japan, Park Jung-hee made a declaration on October 17.

*martial law: When military authorities declare rule over a nation under a state of emergency.
*October Reformation: It was emergency statement declared by Park Jung-hee on Oct. 17, 1972. He did this to remain in power indefinitely.

Dae-jung traveled to the U.S. and Japan to tell everyone about the military's corruption and the people's fight for democracy in Korea. International society began to know about the Korean situation. The world began to call Dae-jung 'the hope of Korean democracy.'

Naturally, the Park Jung-hee regime did not like what Dae-jung was doing. On August 8, 1973, Dae-jung was kidnapped on his way to attend an assembly.

SPLASH
SPLASH
Am I on a ship?
Dae-jung thought that he was going to be killed on the sea.
Oh, no!
So, this is the end of my life.
But I have things I must do for people.

It was discovered that a secretary from the Korean Embassy was related to the kidnapping incident. As it became known to the international society, Dae-jung was released near his home after 129 hours of confinement.

Dae-jung was put under house arrest* under the supervision of police.

This was the only solution the dictating regime had for dealing with Dae-jung. No one was allowed into the house except for his children and wife.

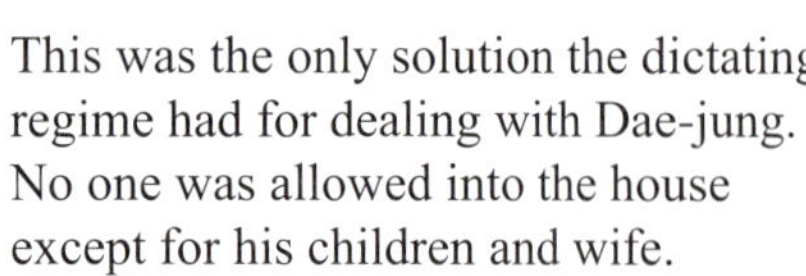

Despite being held captive, Dae-jung continued to do all he could to promote democracy.

*house arrest: If someone is under house arrest, they are officially ordered not to leave their home.

Going to work? But you are under house arrest. We are surrounded by police.
Work can be done at home. I am going to the library room to work.

Actually, I don't want to feel trapped, so I've decided to put on my suit and work as if I were a free man.

That's nice, dear. Let's not lose hope.

Every day, Dae-jung would put on his suit and go into his library to work.

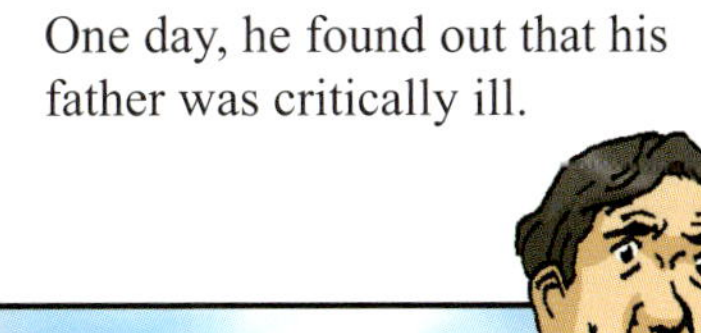

One day, he found out that his father was critically ill.
Please let me go! I need to see my father before he dies!

No, don't forget that you are under arrest!

How would you feel if you were in my situation? You must have parents as well! Please let me go!

I am sorry but we are under strict orders. We can't let you go.

His requests were ignored and it wasn't long before he heard news that his father had died.

I need to be at my father's funeral at least. Can't you let me go?

But the regime did not even allow him to go to his own father's funeral.

Oh... Father... I am so sorry, Father!

The dictatorship was becoming worse. An emergency declaration was made in 1974.

Release Kim Dae-jung!

The students demonstrated more actively against the government. On March 2, 1976, Dae-jung and scholars made a declaration for democracy.

Dae-jung was imprisoned for two years and ten months for this incident.

People didn't stop fighting for democracy. On October 26, 1979, Park Jung-hee was assassinated by Kim Jae-gyu, the Director of the KCIA. The 17-year long regime finally ended.

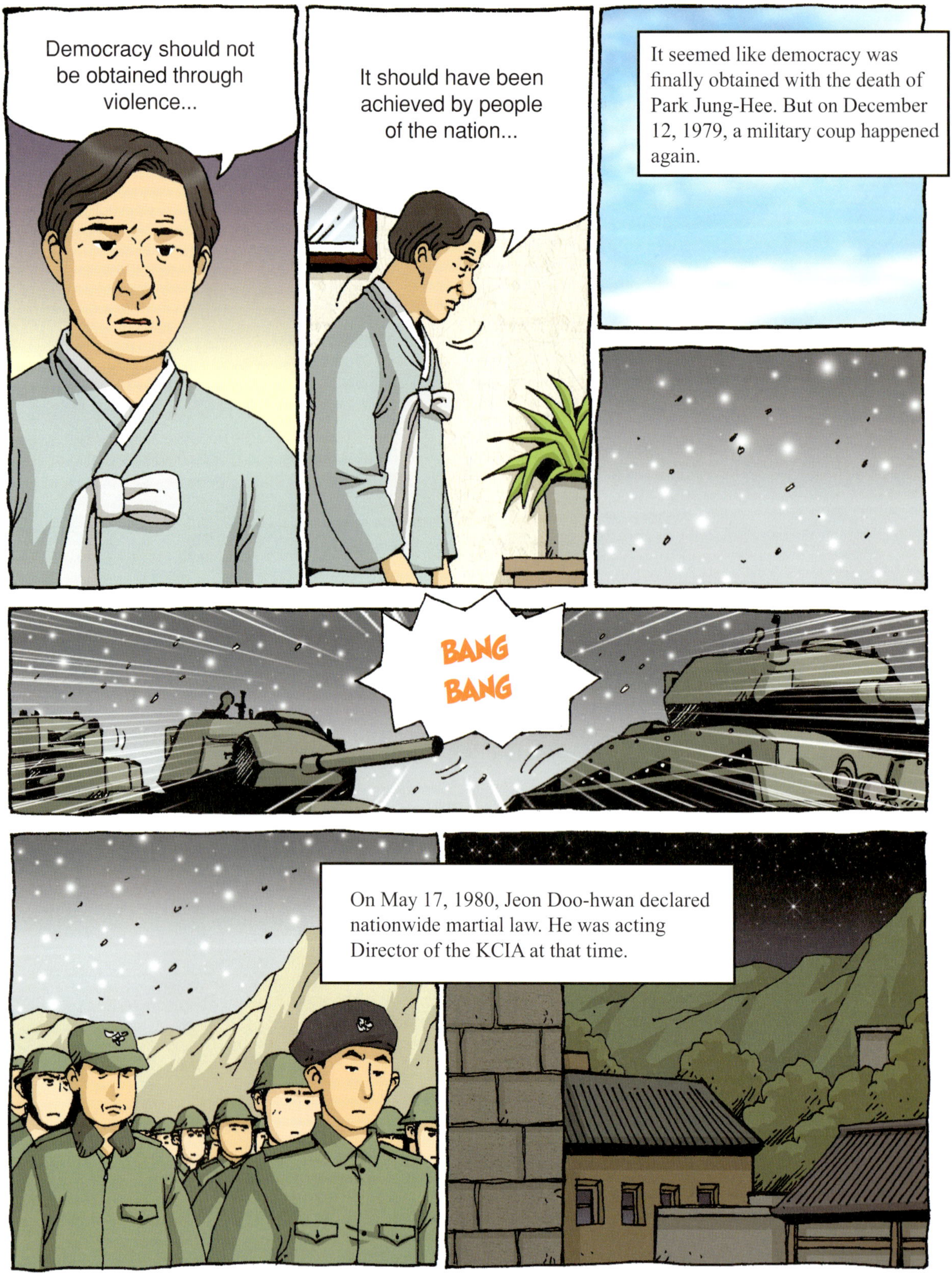

Democracy should not be obtained through violence...

It should have been achieved by people of the nation...

It seemed like democracy was finally obtained with the death of Park Jung-Hee. But on December 12, 1979, a military coup happened again.

BANG BANG

On May 17, 1980, Jeon Doo-hwan declared nationwide martial law. He was acting Director of the KCIA at that time.

*new military regime: It is a military regime of Korea that overtook the military regime of Park Jung-Hee. Although they are of similar nature, the new name was provided to distinguish it from the previous regime.

The defendant may make a final speech.
When this nation stands on the legs of true democracy, let there be no more political revenge.
701

His family members, foreign press reporters and public workers were at the court that day.
He made a slow but clear speech, which was reported worldwide.
Hmm...
The trial attracted worldwide attention. The entire progress was reported real-time.

The defendant is guilty, and is sentenced to death.
BANG BANG BANG
Oh, no!
Ah!
Sob... Sob...

The court was filled with tears when his sentence was declared.
Until that day~
When the waters of the Eastern Sea~
People at the court began to sing the National Anthem in tears.
Run dry and Mt. Baekdu is worn away~
May god protect and preserve...
...our nation~

A Prepared President

 Track 13 ▶

Dae-jung was a symbol of democracy. International media and famous people around the world put pressure on the Korean government. The Secretary of State from the U.S. made a statement saying that, "We deeply regret the sentence which was declared on Kim Dae-jung." President Reagan proclaimed that the U.S. government would recognize Jeon Doo-hwan as acting president if the sentence was taken back.

Willy Brandt from Germany passed a vote in Germany to save Dae-jung. International democracy associations and organizations campaigned to save Dae-jung.

Dae-jung was imprisoned at Chungjoo Jail on January 31, 1961. He was kept alone in a small and cold cell.

He spent his time writing letters to his family and reading many books.

Only one paper for a letter was allowed a month. He had to write the letters with very small characters. When he became good at this, he was able to write 14,000 characters on a piece of paper. Later on, 29 of these letters would be published in a book.

After lunchtime he was allowed to exercise for an hour every day. He tended flowers during that time.

Even prison guards began to help him tend flowers in the end.

You are very honest creatures. You grow when you are watered. And you become stronger if I care for you honestly.

Why are these flowers withering? Please understand that I care for you. I am doing my best.

My joint inflammation is getting worse... I guess I am getting old.
Dae-jung's sentence was commuted to 20 years of imprisonment on March 1, 1982. He was finally released on December of the same year. But his health had become terrible because of poor conditions in the prison.
Welcome back.
It must have been hard for you.
We cannot do anything in this country anymore. They told me that they will release other innocent people if we chose to be exiled. Let's move to the U.S.

Yes, let's stay there until I get better.

The entire family of Dae-jung moved to the U.S. on December 23, 1982. It was only possible because democratic countries around the world had pressured President Jeon Doo-hwan.

Dae-jung worried about Korea even when he was in the U.S.

He established the Korean Human Rights Research Center to fight for democracy in Korea. He made speeches wherever he was needed. He told everyone about the political situation of Korea.

I can't do much here in the U.S. I must return to Korea.

The general elections will start soon. If I can help, I must go back. My friends are waiting for me.

Dae-jung decided to return to Korea. People around him tried to stop him. They were worried that President Jeon Doo-hwan would not want him back but Dae-jung was willing to risk his life for democracy.
Sir, we cannot guarantee your safety if you return to Korea.
They will try to put you in jail again.
It is not the time yet. You should wait until the situation becomes better.
If I die, I shall die in my own nation. This is my decision.
Korea is where I belong and I must fight for the good of the nation.

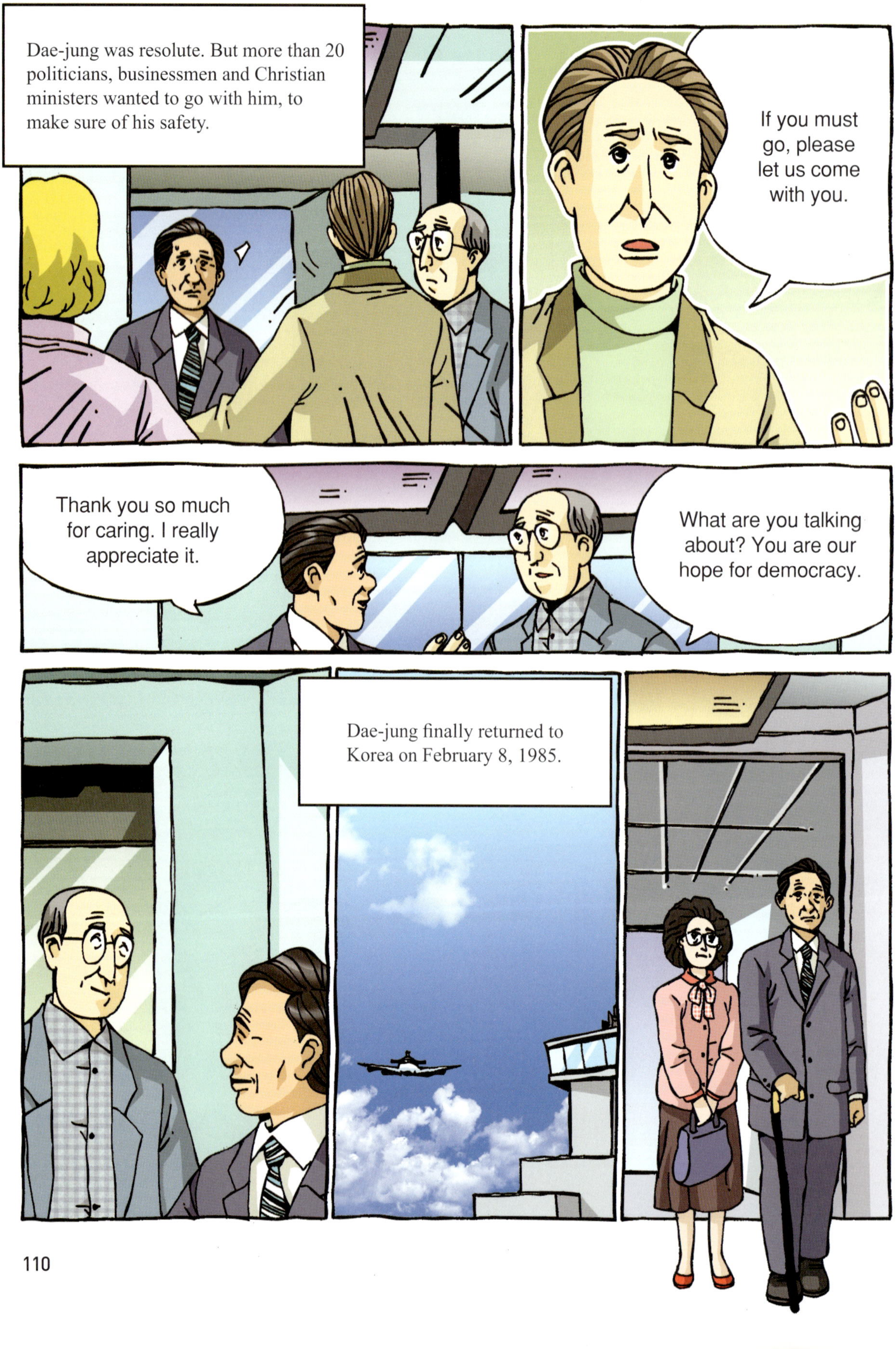

Dae-jung was resolute. But more than 20 politicians, businessmen and Christian ministers wanted to go with him, to make sure of his safety.

Welcome back Mr. Kim!
Our hope for democracy is back!
He makes us proud!
Kim Dae-jung!
The Korean people hadn't forgotten him. His eyes were filled with tears when he was welcomed back by large crowds and the media. .
I am sorry that I had to leave. I am what I am because the Korean people supported me the most.
I promise you that I will bring democracy to Korea.

Fighting for democracy became more intense after Dae-jung returned.

Dae-jung was the people's best hope for democracy. He cried for democracy and direct presidential elections.

No More Dictatorship

What is this smell?

It's tear gas!

Go home! If you don't break up, you are all going to be arrested!

At first, students began demonstrating but soon, everyone began to join. The new military regime tried to suppress people but it only made people angrier.

Help! This man has been shot by a tear gas bullet!

Demonstrations began to get more intense. A student from Yonsei University, Lee Han-yeol, was killed.

The people were outraged. 1.5 million people participated in demonstrations nationwide. The new military regime began to fear the people.

Step down from power! Bring democracy to Korea! Let us have direct presidential elections!

The president was elected through an indirect election system. People could not participate in the elections at that time.

On June 29, 1987, the 6.29 Declaration was made. The government accepted the people's requests. They agreed for direct presidential elections and granted amnesty to Dae-jung.

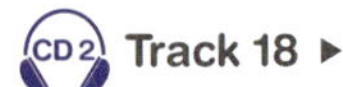

We accept the people's requests. We shall put on direct presidential elections. We also grant amnesty to Kim Dae-jung and permit him political activities.
The new military regime finally gave in on June 29, 1987. the Korean people had finally obtained power to decide the fate of the nation.
Hurray! Hurray! We finally have democracy in our nation!
Vote for Kim Dae-jung!
Dae-jung ran for the elections on the same year. People were excited to experience true democracy.

But it was Roh Tae-woo who won the elections in the end. He was the only candidate of the opposing party. The votes for Kim Dae-jung's party had been split towards three different candidates.
It was my fault for being too stubborn.
I should have stepped down. Then all votes would have added up to win the election.
In 1992, he ran for presidential elections again but failed to win yet again.
Dae-jung accepted this defeat and he finally made up his mind.

Dear, don't be too disappointed.
What do you mean?
It was the people's decision. I am not disappointed.
I think it is time for me to retire. I am thinking about stepping down from politics. What do you think?
People may not understand your dreams yet. But what you have done will be recorded in history. I am happy with any decision you make.

Dear fellow citizens! I have once again failed to get your trust.
I am going to put an end to my political career, to which I dedicated 40 years of my life.
I deeply regret not being able to show you a brighter future.
I would like to leave everything behind me and become an ordinary citizen myself.
After 40 years of hardship, Dae-jung's dream of bringing justice to politics had seemed to come to an end. The press conference hall was filled with tears.

Dae-jung retired and went to Cambridge as a visiting scholar.

Dae-jung did not have grand plan when he left Korea this time. He spent time reading and preparing lectures.

But he realized what he must do when he saw the unification of Germany.

He realized what was needed in Korea when he saw the collapsed walls of Berlin. He decided to dedicate the rest of his life to the unification of Korea.

The walls dividing Korea should collapse like these walls.

South and North Korea must collaborate and understand each other to achieve unification. But it won't be easy. We must work hard to achieve unification.

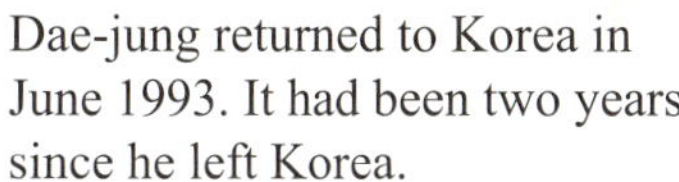

Dae-jung returned to Korea in June 1993. It had been two years since he left Korea.

He established the Peace Foundation for the Asia Pacific Region right after he returned to Korea. It was a foundation for the peaceful development of democracy in Asia.

During this time, the Korean peninsula was under the threat of North Korea's nuclear program. The U.S. wanted to inspect for nuclear weapons. But North Korea didn't allow this.

North Korea continued to develop nuclear warheads and the U.S. prepared to attack nuclear facilities in North Korea.

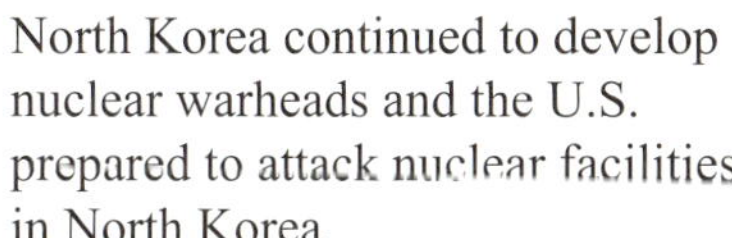

Yes, it is.
North Korea and the U.S. are too stubborn.
The South Korean government doesn't know what to do.
It wouldn't have been this bad if he was the president.
Who are you talking about?
Who do you think? I'm talking about Kim Dae-jung.

The government did not have a clear solution to the conflict and people were getting weary of the situation.

Dae-jung felt that someone should step in before a war broke out again.

The man from Aesop's fables clutches his coat when the wind blows strong. But he takes off his coat with warm sunshine.

North Korea would agree to a summit meeting if we show them kind warmth instead of cold threats.

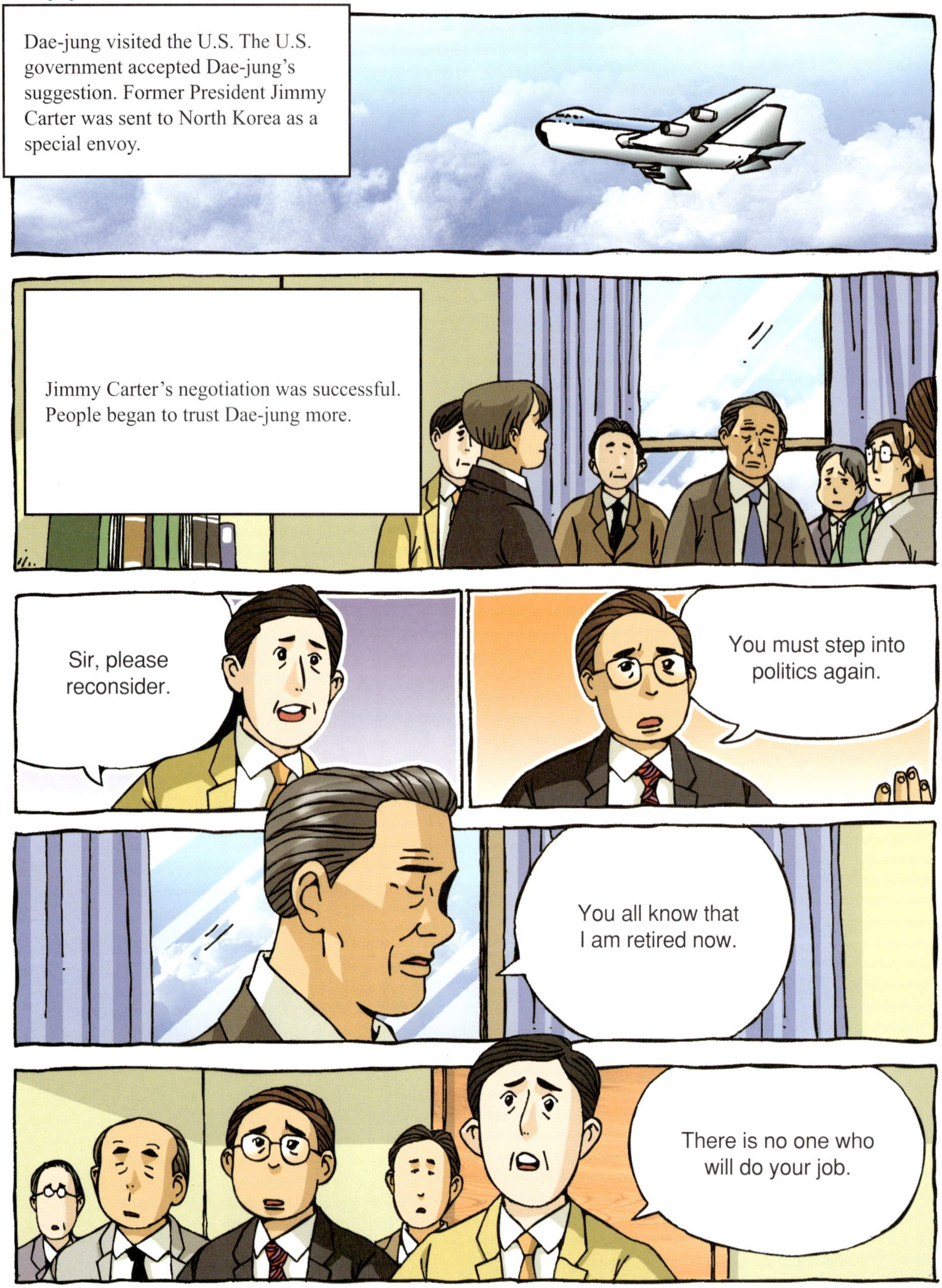

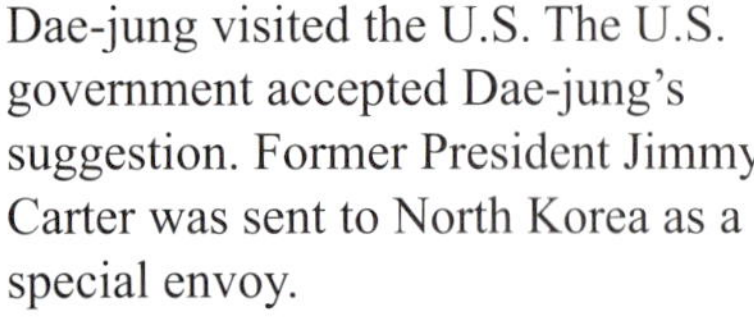

Dae-jung visited the U.S. The U.S. government accepted Dae-jung's suggestion. Former President Jimmy Carter was sent to North Korea as a special envoy.

Jimmy Carter's negotiation was successful. People began to trust Dae-jung more.

I can't go against the people's wishes. There are many policies that must be changed, and I am still passionate for peace and democracy. Yes... I shall sacrifice for Korea once more.
Dae-jung returned to politics.
He ran for the election under the slogan 'A Prepared President.' On December 18, 1997, he finally become the 15th President of Korea.
Kim Dae-jung!
Kim Dae-jung!
Hurray for President Dae-jung!
It was a historical moment. It was the first time a regime had changed peacefully in Asia. Korea became a model of democracy in Asia through this election.

The Star Shines for the Last Time

Dae-jung faced a national crisis as soon as he became President. It was the Asian financial crisis in 1997. The economy of Korea was in crisis and regulations needed to be changed.

Dae-jung did not have time to waste. The biggest problem was the financial crisis. Korea had run out of foreign currency at that time. Korean companies desperately competed with each other to get this foreign currency to buy imported goods. This eventually made the Korean Won drop and the US dollar to rise in value. The Korean government had no choice but to ask for a relief loan worth 20 billion dollars from the International Monetary Fund.

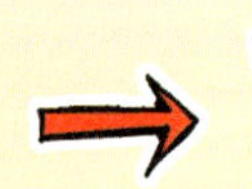

But the IMF wanted to interfere with the Korean economy through this relief loan.
The Korean government had to come up with a way to be free from the interference. The only way was to pay off the debt. The government and people worked together to take care of the problem.
Gold prices are rising internationally. Let's plan a campaign to collect gold donation.
People began to contribute to the debt collection by donating gold. Everyone around the nation contributed gold for the crisis.

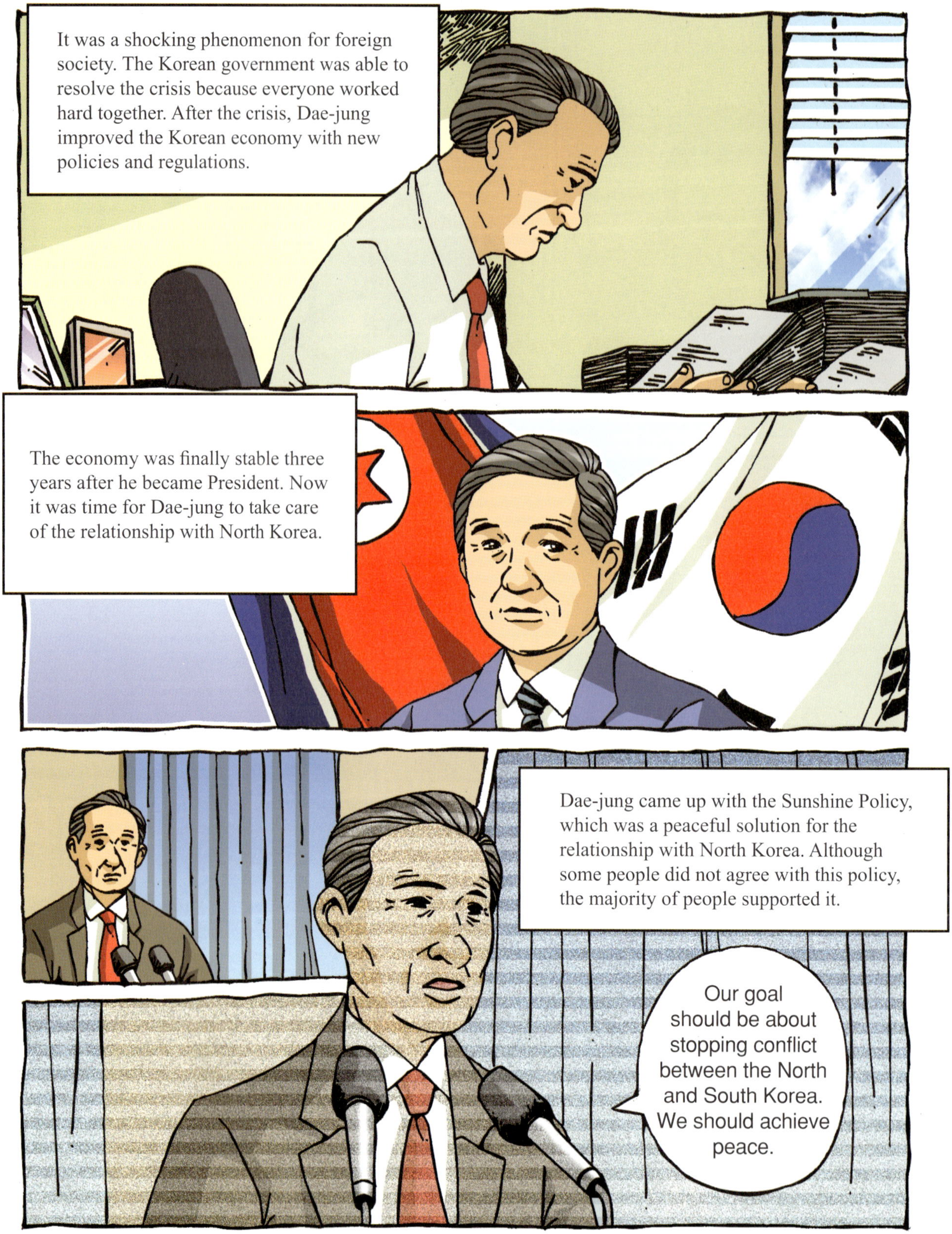

It was a shocking phenomenon for foreign society. The Korean government was able to resolve the crisis because everyone worked hard together. After the crisis, Dae-jung improved the Korean economy with new policies and regulations.

The economy was finally stable three years after he became President. Now it was time for Dae-jung to take care of the relationship with North Korea.

Dae-jung came up with the Sunshine Policy, which was a peaceful solution for the relationship with North Korea. Although some people did not agree with this policy, the majority of people supported it.

We need to show North Korea friendship and generosity. We need to help North Korea.
We are going to help North Korea as much as we can to make a brighter future for both nations.
I trust Kim Dae-jung.
Think about everything he has done for this nation so far.
The unification will happen soon because of him.
The North and South should collaborate for peaceful unification.
Let us work hard for a brighter future of a united Korea.

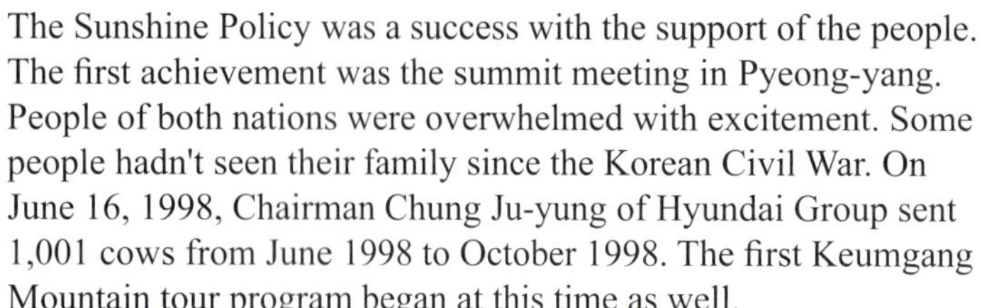

The Sunshine Policy was a success with the support of the people. The first achievement was the summit meeting in Pyeong-yang. People of both nations were overwhelmed with excitement. Some people hadn't seen their family since the Korean Civil War. On June 16, 1998, Chairman Chung Ju-yung of Hyundai Group sent 1,001 cows from June 1998 to October 1998. The first Keumgang Mountain tour program began at this time as well.

On June 13, 2000, a historic summit meeting was held in Pyeongyang. It was the first summit meeting in 55 years. Kim Jeong-il of the North Korean totalitarian regime met Kim Dae-jung of South Korea.

This was broadcasted on live TV. Many Pyeongyang citizens came out to greet Kim Dae-jung.
Welcome, you have come a long way.
I fear nothing. It is a historical day today.
And they presented a joint announcement after two days.

His visit to North Korea was a big issue worldwide. He was selected as the most influential leader in Asia in 1999.

In October 2000, he was awarded with the Nobel Peace Prize for his dedication to human rights and for bringing peace to the Korean peninsula. It was the first Nobel Peace Prize of the 21st century.

Korean people were very proud. Many influential leaders and figures sent him congratulatory messages.

On December 8, 2000, Kim Dae-jung and his wife went to Oslo to attend the award ceremony.

The ceremony was filled with sunflowers and many other yellow flowers, which represented his Sunshine Policy.

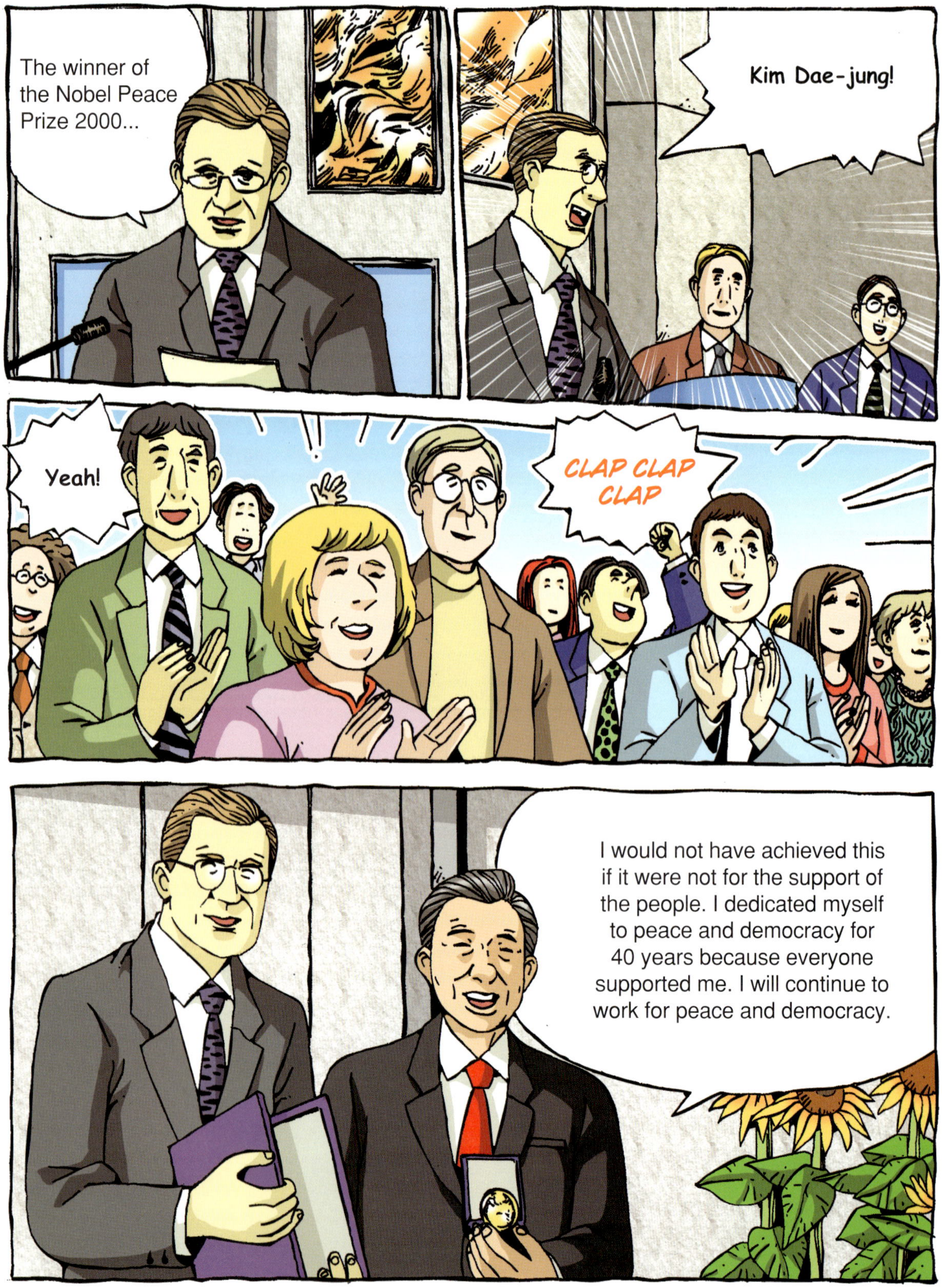

The winner of the Nobel Peace Prize 2000...
Kim Dae-jung!
Yeah!
CLAP CLAP CLAP
I would not have achieved this if it were not for the support of the people. I dedicated myself to peace and democracy for 40 years because everyone supported me. I will continue to work for peace and democracy.

His term in office ended two years later in February 2003.
He had already achieved so much by the time his term was finished. But he continued to travel to Europe, Malaysia, China, the U.S., Japan and other nations to make speeches and attend lectures.
When he was free, he spent time reading books.

His health was getting worse from injuries and illnesses he had gotten from his torture and imprisonments.
I knew you would be here reading books. How about we go out to get some air?
They are so beautiful aren't they?
I think you are the most beautiful thing here.
You must be joking, I am too old. It's been more than 40 years since I married you.

Cough!

Are you alright?

I am fine.

I thought I would always be young when I was fighting for democracy. I guess I am too old as well.

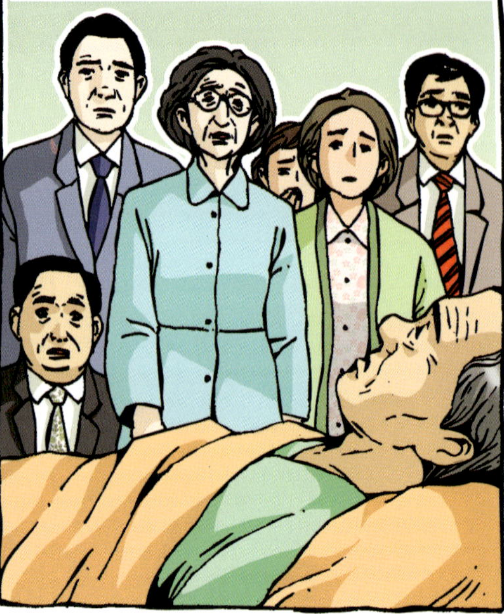
Dae-jung died from pneumonia on August 18, 2009. His family was present to say their final goodbyes to him.

No, dear!
A state funeral was held with people from all around the world attending to pay tribute to him.

Kim Dae-jung never stopped fighting for democracy even when his life was threatened. He fought against vicious dictatorships and brought true democracy to Korea.

He was often hurt by the media and politics, but he always fought for justice and never looked for an easy way out. He went through hardships all his life but he embraced everything with patience and love.

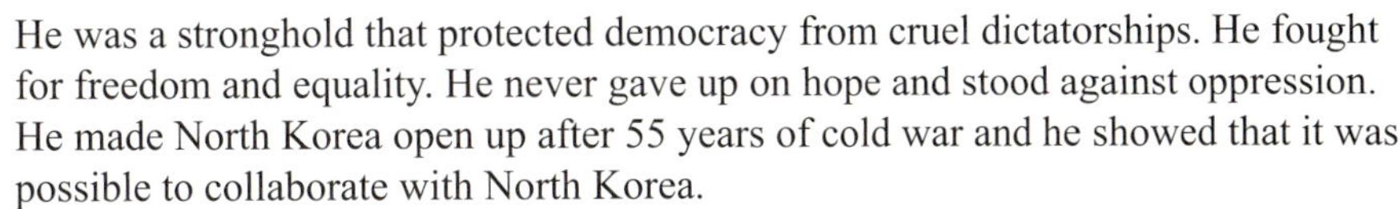

He was a stronghold that protected democracy from cruel dictatorships. He fought for freedom and equality. He never gave up on hope and stood against oppression. He made North Korea open up after 55 years of cold war and he showed that it was possible to collaborate with North Korea.
He dedicated himself not only to the peace of Korea but the peace of the world. Today, the Korean people continue to cherish his strong beliefs in democracy and peace which he fought so hard to give them.

I believe that peaceful prosperity cannot be achieved in Korea without unification. We have been one nation for over 1,000 years ever since the days of Shilla Kingdom. Compared to that, our divided history is only a short time of the history.

- *Excerpt from the Biography of Kim Dae-jung.*

Word Search

● Find the words which are hidden horizontally, vertically and diagonally.

```
S M Z G Q M Z G Q M Z G Q J M Z G Q M X
W O I N A E N T I O N H W I N C H C R O
E B M J A B Q J E T E A R B A O I O E M
R V C P R D C K R V V K G R V M K M C F
E C T O A S E N T C A L T T C M U K O E
V X E Q Y N P O Y X N Q Y Y Y X U N O N M
E S A C R I F I C E M W R I Z N J N C W
A N A E I A E O I A E Z E N A I A E I I
L I N D E P E N D E N T H J S S S R L T
G D C U P D H T O D I E O U D T T B L P
A F A Y H F U Y A T C Y V S F U Y I A L
S G S U S T I N C R A G E T N G U T T A
T H S I D H M I D H L I R I H O I Y I U
O P A B S O R A F J T J P C J T J F O S
R A N P R M N O R T I O N E T E B G N X
H T A N H L E N H E E N H H A E N H L B
J I T M J Q T A U T D O R I T C M J B L
L E E Q L W Y Q L W Y Q L N W Y E L U E
Z N R E H E N T Z B K F Z M S U F T J R
X C O N S T I T U T I O N T U R E X N M
W E Q F C R Q C P R O P H X R Q C V R P
```

constitution	peace	reconciliation	sacrifice
patience	communist	independent	injustice

Vocabulary

● Match each word to the correct meaning.

1. patriotic	• 독재
2. authoritative	• 투옥
3. courage	• 애국적인
4. politician	• 권위적인
5. election	• 통일
6. dictatorship	• 용기
7. demonstration	• 사면
8. democracy	• 선거
9. congress	• 의회
10. imprisonment	• 시위
11. unification	• 정치가
12. amnesty	• 민주주의

3 Guess What?

● Guess what she said in the blank.

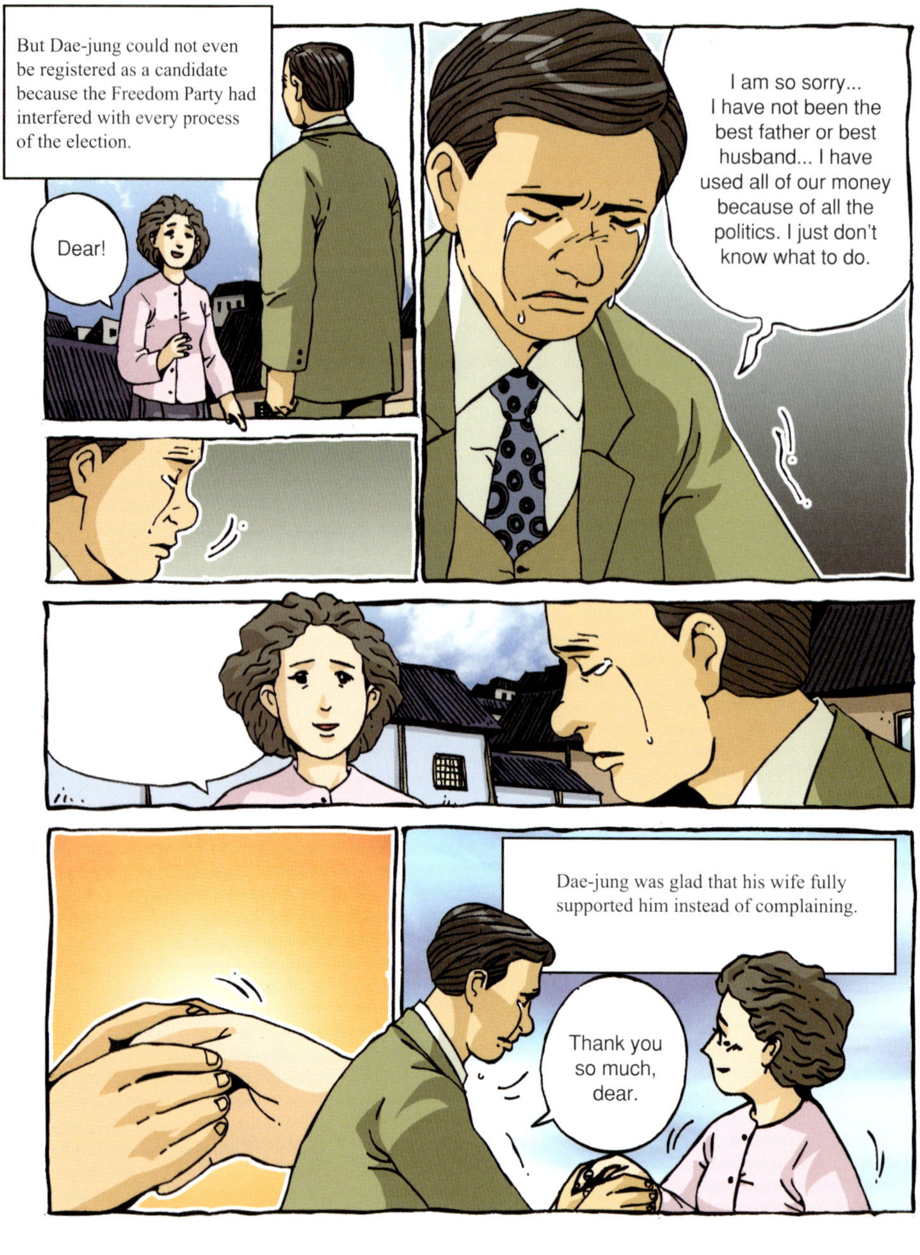

The Symbol of Korea

Think about an example of a Korean Symbol. Draw your Korean symbol in the box below and write why you think it represents Korea.

About Korea

● Check out how much you know about Korea.

1. Write consonant letters of Korean alphabet starting with 'ㄱ.'

____

2. Write five Korean cuisines.

____

3. Write five Korean islands.

____

4. Write five Korean famous mountains.

____

5. Write five Korean famous rivers.

____

6. Write five Korean traditional games.

____

7. Write five Korean traditional musical instruments.

____

8. Write five Korean former Presidents.

____

9. Write five Korean movies or dramas in English titles.

____

10. Write five words describing Korea and Korean people.

____

About Koreans

● Check out how much you know about Korean people.

1. Korean people are good at ____.

2. Korean people are poor at ____.

3. Korean people like to ____.

4. Korean people dislike to ____.

5. Korean people usually want to have ____.

6. Korean children are ____.

7. Korean mothers are ____.

8. Korean fathers are ____.

9. Koreans are cool because ____.

10. I am a ____ Korean.

연표

1924년   1월 6일, 전라남도 신안군 하의면 하의도에서 태어났습니다. 1943년에 일제의 징병을 피하기 위해 1925년 12월 3일로 출생일을 정정합니다.

1933년 9세   서당에서 한학을 배웠습니다.

1936년 12세   목포로 이사하여 목포제일공립보통학교로 전학했습니다.

1945년 21세   차용애와 결혼합니다.

1954년 30세   3대 민의원 선거에서 무소속으로 목포에 출마해 떨어졌습니다.

1956년 32세   명동성당에서 세례를 받았습니다. 세례명은 토머스 모어입니다.

1959년 35세   제4대 민의원 선출을 위한 강원도 인제 재선거에서 낙선합니다. 부인 차용애가 병으로 사망합니다.

1961년 37세   민주당 대변인으로 임명됩니다. 제5대 민의원 보궐 선거에 출마해 당선되지만 5·16 쿠데타로 이틀 만에 의원직을 빼앗깁니다.

1962년 38세   이희호와 재혼합니다.

1963년 39세   제6대 국회의원 선거에서 목포에 출마해 당선됩니다.

1971년 47세   제7대 대통령 선거에서 낙선합니다.

1973년 49세   도쿄에서 납치되어 129시간 만에 동교동 자택으로 돌아옵니다. 가택 연금을 당하고 모든 정치 활동을 금지당합니다.

1976년 52세   재야 민주 지도자들과 함께 3·1 민주 구국 선언을 주도합니다.

1977년 53세	대법원에서 징역 5년 형이 확정됩니다.
1980년 56세	신군부의 비상계엄령이 전국으로 확대되면서 내란 음모 혐의를 받아 연행됩니다. 내란 음모 혐의로 군사 재판에서 사형 선고를 받습니다.
1981년 57세	사형에서 무기형으로 감형됩니다.
1982년 58세	무기형에서 20년으로 감형됩니다. 형 집행 정지로 석방되어 미국으로 출국합니다.
1987년 63세	제13대 대통령 선거에서 낙선합니다.
1988년 64세	제13대 국회의원에 당선됩니다.
1992년 68세	제14대 국회의원에 당선됩니다. 제14대 대통령 선거에서 낙선합니다. 정계 은퇴를 선언합니다.
1994년 70세	아시아·태평양 평화재단을 설립합니다.
1995년 71세	정계 복귀를 선언합니다. 새정치국민회의를 창당합니다.
1997년 73세	제15대 대통령에 당선됩니다.
1998년 74세	2월 25일, 대통령에 취임합니다.
2000년 76세	6월 13일, 평양에서 남북 정상 회담을 개최합니다. 12월 10일 노벨 평화상을 수상합니다.
2003년 79세	제15대 대통령에서 퇴임한 후 동교동으로 돌아옵니다.
2009년 85세	8월 18일, 세상을 떠났습니다.

who? 01	Barack Obama	979-11-5639-023-7
who? 02	Charles Darwin	979-11-5639-024-4
who? 03	Bill Gates	979-11-5639-025-1
who? 04	Hillary Clinton	979-11-5639-026-8
who? 05	Stephen Hawking	979-11-5639-027-5
who? 06	Oprah Winfrey	979-11-5639-028-2
who? 07	Steven Spielberg	979-11-5639-029-9
who? 08	Thomas Edison	979-11-5639-030-5
who? 09	Abraham Lincoln	979-11-5639-031-2
who? 10	Martin Luther King, Jr.	979-11-5639-032-9
who? 11	Louis Braille	979-11-5639-033-6
who? 12	Albert Einstein	979-11-5639-034-3
who? 13	Jane Goodall	979-11-5639-035-0
who? 14	Walt Disney	979-11-5639-036-7
who? 15	Winston Churchill	979-11-5639-037-4
who? 16	Warren Buffett	979-11-5639-008-4
who? 17	Nelson Mandela	979-11-5639-009-1
who? 18	Steve Jobs	979-11-5639-010-7
who? 19	J. K. Rowling	979-11-5639-011-4
who? 20	Jean-Henri Fabre	979-11-5639-012-1
who? 21	Vincent van Gogh	979-11-5639-013-8
who? 22	Marie Curie	979-11-5639-014-5
who? 23	Henry David Thoreau	979-11-5639-015-2
who? 24	Andrew Carnegie	979-11-5639-016-9
who? 25	Coco Chanel	979-11-5639-017-6
who? 26	Charlie Chaplin	979-11-5639-018-3
who? 27	Ho Chi Minh	979-11-5639-019-0
who? 28	Ludwig van Beethoven	979-11-5639-020-6
who? 29	Mao Zedong	979-11-5639-021-3
who? 30	Kim Dae-jung	979-11-5639-022-0